"In this volume, we are treated to a [...] topic in theology. Matz and Thornhill have assembled a capable group of scholars who not only provide a stimulating set of perspectives on this issue but who do so with winsomeness and grace. An excellent addition to the Spectrum series!"
Paul Rhodes Eddy, professor of biblical and theological studies, Bethel University

"The doctrine of divine impassibility—in some form or other—is an inheritance of the Christian tradition. It is also the subject of much disagreement and debate within recent theology. In this book, this debate is carried forward in a vigorous and very spirited manner as arguments are made from biblical and philosophical theology even as pastoral and experiential concerns are weighed. Anyone interested in the current state of evangelical theological debates about the doctrine of God will find this work enlightening."
Thomas H. McCall, professor of biblical and systematic theology, Trinity Evangelical Divinity School, professorial fellow in exegetical and analytic theology, University of St. Andrews

"Rigorous engagement with the doctrine of divine impassibility has experienced something of a resurgence in recent years. Though perhaps unfamiliar to many laypersons, the various assessments of this doctrine are of no little consequence to our faith and practice. The editors of this volume have assembled a premier group of authors, who in conversation with one another have done a fine job of introducing and spelling out many of the aspects of the contemporary debate over divine impassibility in a manner that is not only lively and stimulating but also broadly accessible. Each of the four authors adeptly unpacks the herme-neutical, methodological, philosophical, historical, and theological commit-ments undergirding his perspective. In tracking those arguments, readers will not only gain a better understanding of each perspective on divine (im)passi-bility but they will also observe how each view intersects with other key doc-trines and proposes practical benefits to our growth as Christians. The editors and authors of *Divine Impassibility: Four Views of God's Emotions and Suffering* have performed a great service in making this conversation available. I am not aware of a better on ramp for getting up to speed on the current discussion than this volume."
Rob Lister, associate professor of theology, Talbot School of Theology, Biola University, La Mirada, CA

"The doctrine of divine impassibility, according to which God is without passions and without emotional change, has a long and distinguished history. Yet it has been subject to sustained criticism in much of modern theology. Does God feel nothing when we suffer? Can such a God be worthy of worship? The editors of this book are to be congratulated for putting into the hands of readers a one-stop-shop overview of this debate. It includes contributions from across the theological spectrum with representative scholars writing in a dialogical format. This way readers quickly get a sense of the central issues in the debate from different perspectives in the discussion. The result is a clearly written symposium from which scholars and students alike will benefit. I heartily recommend it!"

Oliver D. Crisp, Fuller Theological Seminary and the University of St. Andrews

SPECTRUM MULTIVIEW BOOKS

DIVINE
IMPASSIBILITY

FOUR VIEWS OF GOD'S EMOTIONS AND SUFFERING

EDITED BY ROBERT J. MATZ
and A. CHADWICK THORNHILL

Academic
An imprint of InterVarsity Press
Downers Grove, Illinois

InterVarsity Press
P.O. Box 1400, Downers Grove, IL 60515-1426
ivpress.com
email@ivpress.com

InterVarsity Press® is the book-publishing division of InterVarsity Christian Fellowship/USA®, a movement of students and faculty active on campus at hundreds of universities, colleges, and schools of nursing in the United States of America, and a member movement of the International Fellowship of Evangelical Students. For information about local and regional activities, visit intervarsity.org.

Scripture quotations, unless otherwise noted, are from the New Revised Standard Version of the Bible, copyright 1989 by the Division of Christian Education of the National Council of the Churches of Christ in the USA. Used by permission. All rights reserved.

Cover design and image composite: David Fassett
Interior design: Jeanna Wiggins
Images: © The Crucifixion by Odilon Redon at Musee d'Orsay, Paris, France / Bridgeman Images

ISBN 978-0-8308-5253-6 (print)
ISBN 978-0-8308-6662-5 (digital)

Printed in the United States of America ∞

InterVarsity Press is committed to ecological stewardship and to the conservation of natural resources in all our operations. This book was printed using sustainably sourced paper.

Library of Congress Cataloging-in-Publication Data

A catalog record for this book is available from the Library of Congress.

P	25	24	23	22	21	20	19	18	17	16	15	14	13	12	11	10	9	8	7	6	5	4	3	2	1
Y	38	37	36	35	34	33	32	31	30	29	28	27	26	25	24	23	22	21	20	19

To John Morrison,
A wonderful example to us of loving God with all your mind

Contents

Acknowledgments

We would like to first and foremost thank the wonderful contributors who agreed to set their views down on paper for this volume and likewise agreed to be scrutinized by their peers with whom they disagree on this topic. It has been a joy to work with Drs. Castelo, Dolezal, Peckham, and Oord and to have the opportunity to be sharpened by their work. We greatly appreciated their timeliness in responding to inquiries and revisions, and we hope many readers will enjoy the fruits of their labors.

We would also like to thank InterVarsity Press for partnering with us on this project, and particularly David McNutt, who provided insightful and valuable assistance as this project began to take shape. We are also grateful for the work of Ben Forrest who served as the originator of this project but had to step down from it for personal reasons. His work set the initial direction for the volume and we hope he finds it as enjoyable to read as we did to put together.

I (Robert) would like to thank my wife, Jessica, and my children for their love and support. I would also like to thank my colleagues at Midwestern Baptist Theological Seminary for their encouragement in this writing project. I especially want to thank Rustin Umstattd, John Mark Yeats, Matthew Barrett, Sam Bierig, and David Sundeen, who have each in various ways encouraged and contributed to the completion of this work.

I (Chad) would like to thank my wife, Caroline, and my children for their love and support, as well as my wonderful colleagues in the Liberty University School of Divinity who have encouraged me through this and so many other projects.

Introduction

Four Views on Divine (Im)Passibility

ROBERT J. MATZ AND A. CHADWICK THORNHILL

Impassibility, what's that?

This book considers four views on a topic that many Christians may have never given significant thought to: the emotional life of God. Every time we speak of God's love, God's anger, God's jealousy, even God's suffering, we make assumptions about God's emotional life. At first glance, questions about God's emotional life may appear to be speculations similar to questions of how many angels can dance on the head of a pin. After all, on what basis can we even begin to speculate as to how a God who exists independently from his creation emotionally relates with and to his creation?

Yet as we consider the references to God's love, jealousy, anger, and compassion; or ponder what it means for God to be unchanging, distinct from us, and perfect; or reflect on what it means for God to become incarnate as a man, to live, to suffer, and die, we are forced to wrestle with the idea that God reacts and emotes toward us. Yet, if we as the created can bring about such responses within the Creator, how can God be perfect, complete, and full apart from his creation? Would not this imply that God needs us in order to be God? Can such a being even be rightly understood as God? As we consider the question of the passibility and impassibility of God, we consider (in part) what it means for God to be God.

This book presents four theses about what it means for God to be God in relation to himself and to his creation. The first comes from James E. Dolezal (PhD, Westminster Theological Seminary), assistant professor at Cairn

University. He argues for "strong impassibility," according to which God does not experience emotional changes. The second view comes from Daniel Castelo (PhD, Duke University), professor of dogmatic and constructive theology at Seattle Pacific University, who asserts a "qualified impassibility," in which God cannot be affected by an outside force against his own will (implying that God can be affected by that which he wills to be affected by).

In contrast to these first two definitions, the next two views, strong and qualified passibilists, see God as being affected by his creation. John C. Peckham (PhD, Andrews University), professor of theology and Christian philosophy at Andrews University, argues for a "qualified passibility," wherein God experiences emotional change because of his creation. This change, for Peckham, is tempered by God's freedom and omnipotence. Finally, Thomas Jay Oord (PhD, Claremont Graduate University), professor of theology and philosophy at Northwest Nazarene University, argues for "strong passibility," in which humans bring about genuine emotional change within the divine life, causing God to experience the unexpected.

FOUR KEY ISSUES IN THE (IM)PASSIBILITY DISCUSSION

The other day I (Robert) was sharing about the idea of impassibility with a family member. At first, she was uninterested. "Why would anyone care about that? You theologians have way too much time on your hands. You need to quit speculating about vain philosophy and spend more time reading the Bible and experiencing the God of the Bible. Why on earth would you want to put together a book on that? Why on earth would anyone want to read about that?"

"Well," I responded, "I see why at first glance this might seem speculative. Yet this issue affects everything from how we pray to how we worship God. For example, a passible God hurts when we hurt. When we pray to him about something wrong in our life, we understand that he is genuinely affected by our prayers because he understands what it's like for us to hurt. He experiences pain, just as we experience pain."

"You mean there are people who think God doesn't experience pain?" she responded. "That's messed up! How could anyone think that? What about Jesus dying on the cross?"

"You're right, the cross is a big issue in this discussion. But those who think God is impassible make a really good point as well. If God reacts to us, if he hurts because we can make him hurt, is he still the God of the Bible? How is he the all-powerful Creator of heaven and earth, if we can make him react to us? When Jesus suffers, maybe he suffered as a man, but his divine nature was unaffected."

"Huh," she said. "I'd never thought about any of that before. This sounds really complicated. I think I see why there needs to be a book about it. Still, is there a way to make this discussion approachable to people like me?"

My family member is right. This topic at first glance is strange and unapproachable. Often in these theological debates, the practical implications of a theological position is not made explicit, leaving those not immersed in theological inquiry wondering why it matters. As a result, we have requested that each contributor address the following four questions as a part of their articulation of their view to help demonstrate the relevance of this dimension of our view of God.

1. To what extent is God's emotional life analogous to human emotional life?

2. Are God's nature, will, and knowledge passible, and to what extent?

3. Do the incarnation and passion of Jesus Christ necessitate passibility?

4. Does human activity (such as prayer) occasion an emotive/volitional response from God?

We asked contributors to respond to the first question because there are numerous Scripture passages that refer to God experiencing emotions. For example, when the Scriptures speak of God being angry, does that mean he is angry in the same way we are? While each contributor sees the emotive language of God as analogous (that is, corresponding but not identical) to human emotional life, impassibilists emphasize dissimilarity while passibilists emphasize similarity.

The second question deals with how God relates to his creation. Can we as the created bring about suffering and emotional change within God? Or do God's nature, will, and knowledge independent of his creation determine his emotional life? This is pertinent when we think, for example, of God's wrath or love. Is God's love somehow reciprocal, in a give-and-take relationship with humans, or is his love unaffected by human response?

Four Questions for Four Views on Divine Impassibility

	To what extent is God's emotional life analogous (similar and dissimilar) to the human emotional life?	Are God's nature, will, and knowledge passible, and to what extent?
Strong Impassibility	A strong emphasis on the dissimilarity between human emotion and divine emotion. Just as the biblical language of God having body parts (arm, leg, etc.) does not mean God has a literal body, so too with divine emotions. All passion language is anthropopathic.	No. To allow for any form of passibility requires an ontological openness insomuch as the passible subject must be capable of being moved by some determining agent to newly acquired states of being.
Qualified Impassibility	A qualified emphasis on dissimilarity in language. Unlike humans, divine emotional language does not indicate that God can be overwhelmed by an emotion. Rather such language indicates that God experiences emotions voluntarily.	Yes, but God's nature is passible only to the extent that God allows himself to be. God cannot be affected against his will by an outside force.
Qualified Passibility	There is both similarity and dissimilarity with human emotions. God willingly takes on suffering, whereas humans tend to avoid it at all cost. God restrains his anger whereas humans can be controlled by it.	Yes, God's will and nature are passible while his knowledge is impassible. God is voluntarily essentially passible in relation to the world, meaning God freely chose to create this world and freely opened himself up to being affected by this world in a way that does not diminish or collapse the Creator-creature distinction.
Strong Passibility	Strong emphasis on similarity between divine and human emotions. Scripture gives us good reasons to believe that how God self-reveals (emotionally) corresponds with who God truly is.	Yes, God's nature, will, and knowledge are necessarily passible in relation to the world (because of his love).

The third question addresses the issue of God incarnate. Christians uniformly believe that God became human and dwelt among us. Since Christ as a human experienced emotional change and suffered, what does such say of the divine? Was Jesus' divine nature somehow experientially involved in his suffering and death? If so, was the Trinity thereby affected as well?

The final question relates to how we affect God. Does God experience emotional change because of what we do. Prayer provides a useful case study for this. When we pray, does something within God change? Is God stirred to action by our petitions, or does prayer primarily affect the believer's disposition rather than God's?

	Do the incarnation and passion of Jesus Christ necessitate passibility?	Does human activity (such as prayer) occasion an emotive/volitional response from God?
Strong Impassibility	No. The unity of the two natures of the Son does not passibilize the divine nature and does not impassibilize the human nature. Thus, only the human nature is passible.	No. Prayer works not because it changes God, but because it is arranged by God to be efficacious in the realization of God's eternal plan. Prayer does not change God's will, but rather carries out God's will as one of the secondary causes ordained to accomplish the divine plan. God wills that some things come about as a result of or in answer to our petitions, including our salvation. Both the prayer itself and the response are a part of God's plan.
Qualified Impassibility	Only temporarily. The incarnation and resurrected body and ascension of Christ imply impassibility. Yet, this impassibility is qualified by the suffering and cross of Jesus. The passion of Christ implies passibility only within the larger context of an impassible God.	No. God is unaffected (emotionally and volitionally) by prayer. Rather, because God is unaffected and yet was incarnated, only God is in the position to provide the help our world needs, which he would be unable to provide if he were affected by the world.
Qualified Passibility	Yes, the cross shows that God is passible. To think that Christ only suffered in his humanity would imply that the cross involved merely a human sacrifice and a human Savior. Thus, in order to save, both Christ's divine and human natures are passible.	Yes. The Bible consistently and repeatedly portrays human activity as evoking emotional and volitional divine response.
Strong Passibility	Yes. Jesus shows us God as he is. When he relates with others, expresses emotions, feels compassion, and suffers on the cross, he is acting like God.	Yes. Petitioning prayers presuppose not only that our requests affect God but also that God often acts differently as a result. If God is unaffected by what we do, it makes no sense to petition God.

While each contributor has chosen to answer these questions in slightly different ways, they have all answered them. The table titled Four Questions for Four Views on Divine Impassibility offers a summary of their responses. We provide it here both as a means of orientation to their various perspectives and as a help to readers as you work through their chapters. We hope it will help you to see more clearly how the arguments for their respective positions work.

THE HELLENIZATION HYPOTHESIS AND HISTORICAL DEVELOPMENT OF (IM)PASSIBILITY

A major issue in contemporary debates over (im)passibility is what is known as the Hellenization hypothesis. Over the last hundred and fifty years, a group of theologians have argued that the early Christian theologians, apologists, and philosophers were heavily influenced by Greek philosophy and its idea that God is the unmoved mover.[1] As a result, these theologians assert that instead of looking to Greek philosophy, we needed to realize that the biblical text portrays God as experiencing emotions, as suffering—in other words, as passible. As a result, we should embrace a passible understanding of God.

In recent decades, Jürgen Moltmann has stood as the leading advocate of this position. He states:

> Christian theology acquired Greek philosophy's ways of thinking in the Hellenistic world; and since that time most theologians have simultaneously maintained the passion of Christ, God's Son and the deity's essential incapacity for suffering—even though it was at the price of having to talk paradoxically about 'the sufferings of a God who cannot suffer.' But in doing they have simply added together Greek philosophy's apathy axiom and the central statements of the gospel. The contradiction remains—and remains unsatisfactory.[2]

Over the last two decades, many have pushed back on Moltmann's assertion that impassibility was transplanted into the early church. Some have argued that early church history is far from uniform regarding a strong impassibilist understanding of God.[3] Others contend that both the Scriptures and the earlier Christian thinkers rightly understood God as strongly impassible.[4]

---

[1] Adolf von Harnack largely pioneered this thesis in *What Is Christianity?* trans. T. Bailey Saunders and Rudolf Bultmann, Fortress Texts in Modern Theology (Philadelphia: Fortress, 1986), 207, 211-12.

[2] Jürgen Moltmann, *The Trinity and the Kingdom: The Doctrine of God* (Minneapolis: Fortress, 1993), 22. See his prolonged engagement with the Hellenization hypothesis in Jürgen Moltmann, *The Crucified God: The Cross of Christ as the Foundation and Criticism of Christian Theology* (Minneapolis: Fortress, 1993), 267-75.

[3] Daniel Castelo, *The Apathetic God: Exploring the Contemporary Relevance of Divine Impassibility*, Paternoster Theological Monographs (Eugene, OR: Wipf and Stock, 2009); Rob Lister, *God Is Impassible and Impassioned: Toward a Theology of Divine Emotion* (Wheaton, IL: Crossway, 2013); Paul L. Gavrilyuk, *The Suffering of the Impassible God: The Dialectics of Patristic Thought*, Oxford Early Christian Studies (New York: Oxford University Press, 2004), 21-46.

[4] James E. Dolezal, "A Review of Rob Lister, *God Is Impassible and Impassioned*," in *Confessing the Impassible God: The Biblical, Classical, and Confessional Doctrine of Divine Impassibility*, ed. Ron Baines

Normally, those arguing both for and against the Hellenization thesis interact extensively with writings from throughout church history. In so doing, some have attempted to show how various thinkers throughout church history had nuanced understandings of God's (im)passibility.[5] Others have argued that specific historical figures accurately convey the faith once for all delivered to the saints through their writings.[6] As a result, most contemporary treatments of God's (im)passibility devote a significant amount of space to the historical development of the doctrine of (im)passibility and debates over how earlier thinkers approached the idea of God as impassible.

While a full-blown discussion of Cyril, Athanasius, Augustine, Calvin, or the Wesleys (just to name a few notable figures) on the subject of God's (im)passibility would be both fascinating and illuminating, we (the editors) have chosen to exclude that discussion from this volume. Our reasons are threefold: First, such a discussion would cause the size of this volume to balloon. Second, it would obscure a general orientation to the biblical, philosophical, and theological issues surrounding God's (im)passibility. Third, even if historical uniformity existed regarding impassibility, this is of lesser significance (for most) than how to work through the varying biblical texts and resulting philosophical arguments.

Nevertheless, because the issue of origins plays a significant role in this debate, and because we have requested that our four contributors not interact with that dimension, we have chosen to provide a brief overview of the key figures and a few key statements from each in this introduction. While it offers only the briefest orientation to this discussion, our hope is that it will whet your appetite for more reflection on this debate.

DIVINE IMPASSIBILITY IN THE EARLY CHURCH

The question of divine impassibility in modern theology frequently occurs in conversation with other voices in the history of Christian thought. These

---

(Palmdale, CA: Reformed Baptist Academic Press, 2015), 409-10; Renihan et al., "Historical Theology, Survey of the Doctrine of Diving Impassibility: Pre-Reformation Through Seventeenth Century England," in *Confessing the Impassible God: The Biblical, Classical, and Confessional Doctrine of Divine Impassibility*, ed. Ron Baines (Palmdale, CA: Reformed Baptist Academic Press, 2015), 225-52; Thomas G. Weinandy, *Does God Suffer?* (Notre Dame: University of Notre Dame Press, 2000), 83-112.

[5] Recently, Rob Lister has done this extensively in *God Is Impassible and Impassioned*, 64-122.
[6] Weinandy, *Does God Suffer?*, 83-112.

figures from centuries past provide dialogue partners in discussing the question of the constancy of God's nature and emotional life. In the introduction to *The Suffering of the Impassible God*, Paul Gavrilyuk notes that while a move away from strong impassibility has occurred in much modern theology, this is often done in breaking with what is viewed as the dominant patristic position. Gavrilyuk notes, "A standard line of criticism places divine impassibility in the conceptual realm of Hellenistic philosophy, where the term allegedly meant the absence of emotions and indifference to the world, and then concludes that impassibility in this sense cannot be an attribute of the Christian God."[7] In other words, scholars often assume that the Jewish view of God as passible in some sense was left behind for a Hellenistic perspective of an impassible deity as the theologians of the early church integrated Platonic and Hellenistic constructs into Christian belief.[8] In looking at the patristic data, and the contexts in which God's impassibility is discussed, it seems perhaps a more nuanced interpretation is needed.

Though not decisive in the debate, the positions of early church theologians are significant for those attempting to affirm a position in keeping with historic Christian belief. This data is of course but one piece of the overall puzzle, as the biblical texts and other theological and philosophical considerations also enter the conversation. As is often the case with debated issues in Christian theology, evidence for both positions can be garnered both from the Scriptures and from the history of Christian thought. The difficulty then becomes how to mediate the spectrum of that data into a coherent theological position.

The question of impassibility in the early church interfaced with the complex matrix of the collision of Christian, Jewish, and Greco-Roman thought structures, in addition to the spectrum of biblical data, and the complex questions of Christology, Trinity, and the suffering and death of

---

[7]Gavrilyuk, *Suffering of the Impassible God*, 2.

[8]A major focus of Gavrilyuk's argument is that Hellenistic thought itself was more complex than this with both impassible (e.g., Platonic) and passible (e.g., the Greek pantheon) understandings of the divine. Perhaps this is why Gavrilyuk can be cited positively by strong impassibilists, qualified impassibilists, and qualified passibilists. See Baines et al., *Confessing the Impassible God*, 229-36; Castelo, *Apathetic God*, 41; John C. Peckham, *Canonical Theology: The Biblical Canon*, Sola Scriptura, *and Theological Method* (Grand Rapids: Eerdmans, 2016), 233n40.

the Son of God. A whole host of questions and tensions subsequently arose, which the early church theologians felt pressure to address. For example, if the Son alone suffered, how is it that in a unified Godhead, the Son alone can become incarnate and die?[9] Does this then jeopardize the unity of God?[10] If God as Son suffered and died, did this introduce some change to the divine nature? Or, if God is not open to suffering or emotions, what does it mean to speak of God's anger, compassion, grief, or joy? Are analogies to human emotions simply limited or altogether insufficient? And how do the emotions of the Son, such as his cry of dereliction at the cross, factor into one's understandings of the emotions of God?

A few examples from the early church illustrate the complexity of the debate. Early in the second century, Justin wrote that Christians worship the "unbegotten and impassible God" who is not goaded by lust, does not need rescuing by others, and does not experience anxiety, all of which are characteristics Justin likened to the deities of the Greek pantheon.[11] Athenagoras likewise critiqued the gods of the pantheon, since they cannot control their anger or sexual desires, can be wounded, and often behave as badly as, if not worse than, humans.[12] Irenaeus criticized those who ascribe human "affections and passions" to God in the same manner in which they operate in humanity.[13] Likewise, Tertullian affirmed that humanity "has the same emotions and sensations as God has, yet not of the same quality as God has,"[14] and John Cassian suggested God's emotions are analogous to human emotions, yet God himself is without passion.[15] In his *Confessions*, Augustine wrote that though God loves most deeply and is perfectly

---

[9]So Eudoxius, in defense of Arianism, postulated, "Let them answer then how this passible and mortal person could be consubstantial with God who is beyond these things: suffering and death." Quoted in R. P. C. Hanson, *The Search for the Christian Doctrine of God: The Arian Controversy 318-381* (New York: T&T Clark, 1988), 112.

[10]Or, as Noetus framed it, according to Hippolytus, "If therefore I acknowledge Christ to be God; He is the Father himself, if He is indeed God; and Christ suffered, being Himself God; and consequently the Father suffered, for He was the Father Himself" (Hippolytus, *Against Noetus* 2.3-5 in vol. 5 of *The Ante-Nicene Fathers: Hippolytus, Cyprian, Caius, Novatian* [New York: Charles Scribner's Sons, 1903], 224).

[11]Justin, *Apology* 1.25.1-3.

[12]Athenagoras, *Plea for the Christians* 21; 29.

[13]Irenaeus, *Against Heresies* 2.13.3.

[14]Tertullian, *Against Marcion* 2.16, in vol. 1 of *Adversus Maricionem*, ed. Ernest Evans (Oxford, Clarendon Press, 1972), 133.

[15]John Cassian, *Institutes* 8.4.3.

compassionate, he is not wounded by sorrow.[16] These authors thus seek to affirm that God has a genuine emotional life, which is even in some way analogous to that of humans, yet also maintain that his emotions are not uncontrolled like those of the gods who dwell atop Olympus.

These affirmations of God's emotions yet denials of his passibility generally occur in comparison with either the Greco-Roman pantheon or the teachings of the heterodox. Many of the church fathers saw impassibility as a means of exposing the temperamental nature of the Greco-Roman gods.[17] Yet the doctrine also interfaced with issues surrounding Christology. In the first centuries of the church, Docetism (which denied Christ's humanity), modalism (which denied the true distinctness of the Triune persons), Arianism (which denied the eternality and divinity of the Son), and Nestorianism (which has often been described as affirming Christ as having two persons rather than two natures) all challenged what was championed as the orthodox interpretation of the God-man.[18] The question of divine impassibility thus had profound implications for one's understanding of both the nature of the Trinity and in particular the person of Jesus Christ. The scandal of God incarnate provided much fodder for debate for those who challenged the teachings of the orthodox.

Athanasius provides an illustration for how these tensions and the issue of impassibility connected with the Christological controversies. Athanasius argued that the suffering of the Son was not of the "Word" (i.e., the divine nature), but rather the "flesh" (i.e., the human nature), contra the Arians who criticized the coherence of the orthodox position on the matter.[19] If the Son is God, then God suffered on the cross, a proposition the opponents of orthodoxy thought absurd enough to force them to change their thinking on the matter. Likewise, Cyril was certain that the sufferings of the Word were both voluntary and purposeful, "in order that when aroused they might be thoroughly subdued by the power of the Word dwelling in the flesh, the [human] nature thus undergoing a change for the better."[20] In other words,

---

[16]Augustine, *Confessions* 3.2.3.
[17]See also Gavrilyuk, *Suffering of the Impassible God*, 50–51.
[18]See Gavrilyuk, *Suffering of the Impassible God*, 173.
[19]Athanasius, *Against the Arians* 3.29.56.
[20]Cyril of Alexandria, *On John 8*, quoted in Gavrilyuk, *Suffering of the Impassible God*, 164.

according to Cyril, the human nature did not influence the divine, but Jesus' divine nature somehow affected and sanctified his humanity.

The issue of impassibility thus surfaced largely in polemical contexts, first against Greco-Roman and Gnostic opponents, and eventually against heterodox groups that challenged the coherence of the teaching that Jesus both shared in the divine essence and yet suffered and died as a human. Interacting with the patristic data on this matter thus shares some of the same challenges as the biblical texts. The theologian must first develop the contexts of these ancient voices to understand why they were communicating what they were just as they must first develop the contexts of the biblical data on the matter in order to interpret the text of Scripture contextually. From there, the challenge is harmonizing those materials in order to present a biblically and historically informed position on this difficult issue.

While the biblical data may seem to lean primarily (at least numerically) in the direction of passibility, and the patristic data primarily in the direction of impassibility (of some form), a responsible theological construction must not simply proof text its way to a view on passibility or impassibility. A careful and contextual reading of both the church fathers and Scripture is required. This alone, however, will not solve the debate. As the essays of this volume will demonstrate, a host of theological and philosophical considerations also come into play. We trust that what follows will inform the minds of the readers concerning how different streams of present-day Christian traditions interact with the question of God's emotional life, and we likewise pray that what follows will impassion their hearts toward the God whom this volume seeks to explore.

1

Strong Impassibility

JAMES E. DOLEZAL

The strong impassibility doctrine maintains that God is without passions.[1] He neither undergoes affective change nor feels the actions of creatures on himself. Thomas Weinandy provides a succinct summary of the doctrine's core claims: "Impassibility is that divine attribute whereby God is said not to experience inner emotional changes of state, whether enacted freely from within or effected by his relationship to and interaction with human beings and the created order."[2] It is this confession of the unchanging and passionless God that I explicate and commend in this chapter.[3]

The notion of a passionless God undoubtedly will strike many contemporary Christians as absurd and maybe even repugnant. What do we make of the many passages in Holy Scripture that attest to God's love, mercy, jealousy, and wrath? Are they without meaning? How could a God without passions really love us or be genuinely indignant at sin? On the face of it, the strong impassibility doctrine might appear to undermine cherished Christian beliefs about God. Even if one grants that proponents of strong impassibility are well intentioned, are they not rather too clever by half

---

[1] Numerous Protestant confessions affirm that God is "without body, parts, or passions," including the Thirty-Nine Articles of Religion (1563), Westminster Confession of Faith (1647), Savoy Declaration (1658), and the Second London Confession (1677/89). The exact phrasing appears to be the coinage of Archbishop Thomas Cranmer, but it has its roots sunk deeply in the patristic and medieval Christian tradition, both Eastern and Western. For a fine collection of sixteenth- and seventeenth-century Reformed texts treating this doctrine, see Samuel Renihan, ed., *God Without Passions: A Reader* (Palmdale, CA: Reformed Baptist Academic Press, 2015).

[2] T. G. Weinandy, "Impassibility of God," in *New Catholic Encyclopedia*, 2nd ed. (Detroit, MI; Washington, DC: Thomson/Gale, 2003), 7:357.

[3] Historically, there is no recognized "weak" variant of the impassibility doctrine. My defense of impassibility operates on the supposition that no such cogent alternative is genuinely possible.

when their position is so patently opposed to the clear witness of the Bible and to the requisite give-and-take that is involved in every act of love or wrath? These are important questions that the strong impassibility advocate must address. I will have something to say in this connection after I have developed in greater detail the meaning of the classical doctrine together with its biblical and theological foundations.

Despite modern bewilderment or offense taken at the strong account of divine impassibility, historically it commanded wide ecumenical backing, being maintained by the Eastern Orthodox, Roman Catholics, Lutherans, Reformed, Anglicans, Presbyterians, Congregationalists, Baptists, Methodists, and more. Among Protestants, it enjoyed sponsorship from figures as diverse as John Calvin, James Arminius, John Gill, and John Wesley.[4] Of course, the broad historical support by no means fixes the truth of the doctrine, but it should give us occasion to seriously ponder its claims rather than dismiss them out of hand.

A significant underlying concern of the classical impassibility doctrine is to safeguard God's fullness and perfection of being. God cannot be the one whose greatness is beyond measure, and who is the absolute Creator on whom all creatures ultimately depend, if it turns out that he himself depends on his creatures, or on any other cause, for some aspect of his being. Every passible being depends for some feature of its being on whatever object rouses it to new states of affection. A minimally adequate defense of impassibility, then, will need to examine in some detail the unique manner of God's being in order to establish the confession that he is the boundless Creator of heaven and earth and all that is in them and that he is in nowise measured or made to be by the creature.

The Christian tradition provides us with a rather precise metaphysical grammar by which we may speak of God's perfection and fullness of being. The terminology of *act* and *passive potency*, while unfamiliar to many today, are particularly critical to understanding how Christians have traditionally

---

[4]For recent presentations of the classical doctrine from the Eastern Orthodox, Roman Catholic, and Protestant perspectives, see David Bentley Hart, "No Shadow of Turning: On Divine Impassibility," *Pro Ecclesia* 11, no. 2 (2002): 184-206; Thomas G. Weinandy, *Does God Suffer?* (Notre Dame, IN: University of Notre Dame Press, 2000); Ronald S. Baines et al., eds., *Confessing the Impassible God: The Biblical, Classical, and Confessional Doctrine of Divine Impassibility* (Palmdale, CA: Reformed Baptist Academic Press, 2015).

articulated this doctrine. In what follows I will be assimilating these notions to a consideration of certain biblical passages that historically have grounded the impassibility doctrine. By underscoring the importance of impassibility as a necessary entailment of God's pure actuality and total lack of passive potency, I will be locating the significance of the doctrine within a consideration of divine being. Talk about God's possibility or impassibility is, at bottom, talk about divine actuality. By reducing the question to one of divine actuality, adherents and opponents are compelled to maintain either that God is being pure and simple, or that he is becoming in some sense and thus beholden to a cause of his being. For the strong impassibilist, this is what the debate is ultimately about. This approach also constrains one to say that either God loves his creatures with an unbounded act of free and uncaused love, or he loves them with a finite, caused, and mutable love. The true superabundance and limitlessness of divine love can only be maintained by the strong impassibility doctrine.

UNDERSTANDING PASSIONS

In order to better appreciate why strong impassibility denies passions of God, it is necessary to get a basic understanding of what *passion* means and why certain affective states humans experience—such as love, joy, compassion, fear, and anger—are called passions. Beginning with the lexical meaning, we observe that our English term passion comes from the Late Latin word *passio* (from the Latin *patī*), which means to suffer, to submit, to undergo, to experience, or to endure. It has the sense of being acted on and of receiving the action of an agent within oneself. The Latin terms are derived from the Greek words *pathos* and *paschō*, which have essentially the same meaning.[5]

As a *received* state of actuality, every passion produces a change in the subject as the consequent of some agent's action on it. Bernard Wuellner defines passion as "any kind of reception of a perfection or of a privation; being considered as acted on by another; the reception of change in the

---

[5] *Pathos* means "that which is endured or experienced, *suffering*." *paschō* means "*experience, be treated* (π. expresses the passive idea corresponding to ποιέω)" and speaks "of everything that befalls a person, whether good or ill." See "πάθος," and "πάσχω," in *A Greek-English Lexicon of the New Testament and Other Early Christian Literature*, edited by Frederick W. Danker et al., 2nd ed. (Chicago: University of Chicago Press, 1979), 602, 633.

being acted upon; any passing from potency to act."[6] George Klubertanz says passion "is the change received from an agent, considered as taking place in the patient."[7] Thomas Aquinas notes, "Passion is the effect of the agent on the patient."[8] Every passion is a caused state of being into which one is moved by the activity of some agent. For this reason, all passions are finite, dependent, time bound, and mutable states of being. Moreover, to experience passion one must possess a principle of receptivity (i.e., passive potency) by which new actuality is received. That is, one must be moveable or changeable. Metaphysically speaking, a passion is an accident that inheres in a substance and modifies the being of that substance in some way. In existential terms, every experience of passion causes the patient *to be* in some new way.

Passions can be either good or bad. Others can act on us in ways that produce joy or sadness, pleasure or pain. Even the term *suffering*, though commonly associated with the infliction of pain, does not necessarily indicate an experience of anguish or distress.[9] Sometimes we deploy the language of affliction to speak of pleasant passions. Humans *fall* in love and are

---

[6] Bernard Wuellner, *Dictionary of Scholastic Philosophy* (Milwaukee: Bruce, 1956), 88-89.

[7] George Klubertanz, *Introduction to the Philosophy of Being*, 2nd ed. (New York: Appleton-Century-Crofts, 1963), 163. Klubertanz defines an agent as "that which by its activity influences the being of another" and a patient as "that which is affected or being changed by another" (163).

[8] Thomas Aquinas, *Summa Theologiae: Complete English Edition in Five Volumes,* trans. Father Lawrence Shapcote, OP, ed. John Mortensen and Enrique Alarcón (Lander, WY: The Aquinas Institute for the Study of Sacred Doctrine, 2012), Ia-IIae.26.2. Thomas identifies both a general and proper sense of passion: "In its general sense passion is the reception of something in any way at all. . . . In its proper sense passion is used of motion, since action and passion consist in motion, inasmuch as it is by way of motion that reception in a patient takes place" (*Quaestiones disputatae de veritate* 26.1). Thomas believes motion is found properly in bodies and so maintains that "in a passion properly so called it is the body that suffers directly" (*Quaestiones disputatae de veritate* 26.2). He concludes, "Strictly speaking, passion is only in the sense appetitive part" (*Quaestiones disputatae de veritate* 26.3). For a careful treatment of these matters, see Robert Miner, *Thomas Aquinas on the Passions: A Study of* Summa Theologiae *1a2ae 22–48* (New York: Cambridge University Press, 2009). The classical impassibility tradition denies passions of God in both senses.

[9] The word *suffer* derives from a combination of the Latin terms *sub* (under) and *ferre* (to bear, to carry), and means to bear under or to carry something that has come upon one. Whether the suffering is good or bad depends on what exactly has come upon the subject. Over time the term has become increasingly reserved for the bearing of ill. The *Oxford Shorter English Dictionary* offers this as the primary sense: "Have (something harmful or painful) inflicted or imposed upon one; submit to (pain, punishment, death, etc.); undergo, experience, be subjected to, (esp. something unpleasant or painful)." A now more seldom-used meaning is also offered: "Be the object of an action, be acted on, be passive." Both usages share the common idea of receiving action upon oneself.

smitten by the objects of their romantic attraction. One's beloved may even be called one's *crush*. These violent terms speak of the intensity and power with which romantic love sometimes comes upon a person. The agent causing this passion is the one loved insomuch as his or her loveliness is the attractive force that moves the lover into a state of actually loving. My wife's loveliness, for instance, is the efficient cause that draws me to her. My love for her is passionate to just the extent that I am affected and moved by her loveliness. A similar account can be given of the other passions, both good and bad. Each is a state of affective actuality into which one enters through a process of being acted on by some cause and receiving from that cause a new (accidental) state of being.

Passions are only so called because of the manner of their coming on the subject through a process of undergoing and reception of new actuality. If one were to possess the virtues of love, joy, mercy, jealousy, and the like without having undergone an intrinsic affective change produced by the action of some causal agent, then those virtues would not be passions in that case. This does not mean those virtues would be deprived of intensity, vitality, or dynamism. To speak of passionless love, joy, mercy, or jealousy means only that these states did not come upon the subject through the reception of actuality from an efficient cause of being. One person could be passionless because of the lack of love, joy, mercy, or jealousy. Another could be passionless because, although he or she is intensely and dynamically loving, joyful, merciful, or jealous, these states are not the effect of some agent's action on him or her. I will argue later in this chapter that only virtues that are *not* instances of passion can be genuinely unbounded, unchanging, and free in the ultimate sense. Suffice it to say that denying passions of God by no means entails that he is without love, joy, mercy, jealousy, and so forth, but only that these virtues are not in him as the result of the determinative action of a causal agent.

BIBLICAL AND THEOLOGICAL MOTIVATIONS FOR STRONG IMPASSIBILITY

The truth of divine impassibility is most convincingly arrived at through the contemplation of other doctrines. It is a necessary entailment of doctrines such as divine aseity and independence, pure actuality, and simplicity. Each of these teachings rules out the possibility of God receiving new actuality of being, and thus of being patient to the actions of a causal agent on him. Given that all instances of passion are instances of change visited on a patient through the causal action of some agent, God must be impassible. I will consider each of the aforementioned doctrines in turn, giving the lion's share of attention to aseity and independence.

Aseity and independence. Divine aseity (from the Latin *a se*, meaning *of himself*) teaches that God is wholly self-sufficient in all that he is and thus exists independently of all causal influence from his creatures. Herman Bavinck follows John of Damascus in declaring that God is "a boundless ocean of being."[10] He is the fountain of life for all who receive life because he has "life in himself" (Jn 5:26). God's independence is not that of a remote or reclusive deity, but of one who is near to his creatures in self-sufficient beneficence bestowing on us life, breath, and all things (Acts 17:25). Indeed, this may well be the significance of God's unique name Yahweh (Ex 3:15; 6:3) as it relates to his free and benevolent presence among his people (Ex 3:12; 33:19).[11] God, whose very name denotes his fullness of being, is near to us as the giver and sustainer of being. I will focus on three passages in support of this claim.

Romans 11:35-36. Paul writes in Romans 11:35 (citing Job 41:11), "Or who has given a gift to him, / to receive a gift in return?" He goes on to declare why this cannot be done: "For from him and through him and to him are all things. To him be the glory forever. Amen" (Rom 11:36). There is nothing the creature possesses that is not *from* or *of* God. As Creator, God is the absolute source of all caused being—in metaphysical speak, of all caused acts of existence and forms of actuality together with matter. Also, God himself is of himself, though not in the same way creatures are. They are of him as from a cause or principle of being; he is of himself in that he is his own sufficient reason for being. Anselm confesses to God, "You are whatever you are, not through anything else, but through

---

[10]Herman Bavinck, *Reformed Dogmatics*, vol. 2: *God and Creation*, ed. John Bolt, trans. John Vriend (Grand Rapids: Baker Academic, 2004), 151.

[11]The expression *'ehyeh 'asher 'ehyeh* ("I Am Who I Am") in Ex 3:14 appears to be an exposition of the name *Yehvah* "Yahweh" given in Ex 3:15. By this unusual existential name God assures his people of his abundant sufficiency for all that concerns them. It is a free sufficiency without bounds or limitation of being and so utterly dependable.

yourself."[12] We need not look back any further than God for some deeper account of the creature's being or of God's being. Yet if God were subject to passions, then this simply could not be true. Some actuality in God's being would be *from* the creature since all passions are states of actuality produced in patients through the activity of an efficient cause.

Some might object that God allows or ordains the creature to act on God and thus move him to new states of affection or feeling. Jürgen Moltmann, perhaps the foremost advocate of divine passibility in the twentieth century, maintains that God suffers actively, which means "the voluntary laying oneself open to another and allowing oneself to be intimately affected by him; that is to say, the suffering of passionate love."[13] Elsewhere he writes, "If God is not passively changeable by other things like other creatures, this does not mean that he is not free to change himself, or even free to allow himself to be changed by others of his own free will."[14] This has become a favored approach of some recent Calvinist theologians who want to affirm that creatures produce emotive changes in God, but also want to ensure that the absolute origination of this intrinsic change in God does not lie with the creature.[15] From the perspective of strong impassibility, this will not do. First, this formulation must presuppose some lack of being in God and openness to new actuality. Every change brings to the one changed a new state of being not previously possessed. Moltmann's assertion that a suffering God "does not suffer out of deficiency of being, like created beings" is nonsensical.[16] Suffering, *qua* suffering, necessarily involves the reception of action on oneself (i.e., of new actuality) and so requires that the sufferer has lacked some form of being. Second, every change is the effect of some causal activity received in the one changed. One cannot be *affected* by another

---

[12]Anselm, *Proslogion* 12, in *Anselm: Basic Writing*, trans. and ed. Thomas Williams (Indianapolis: Hackett, 2007).

[13]Jürgen Moltmann, *The Trinity and the Kingdom: The Doctrine of God*, trans. Margaret Kohl (San Francisco: Harper & Row, 1981), 23.

[14]Jürgen Moltmann, *The Crucified God: The Cross of Christ as the Foundation and Criticism of Christian Theology*, trans. R. A. Wilson and John Bowden (New York: Harper & Row, 1974), 229.

[15]This appears to be the position of Rob Lister in his book *God Is Impassible and Impassioned: Toward a Theology of Divine Emotion* (Wheaton, IL: Crossway, 2012).

[16]Moltmann, *Trinity and the Kingdom*, 23. Moltmann insists that God is capable "of suffering out of the fullness of his being" (*Crucified God*, 230). This renders the term *suffering* unintelligible insomuch as it evacuates it of any sense of receptivity, of any *bearing under* or *being acted on*. No entity can be full of being and susceptible to suffering at the same moment and in the same respect.

without being causally impacted by that one. Strictly speaking, nothing can be self-caused since causation is the conferral of some actuality already possessed in some fashion by the cause itself and lacking in the one who receives it.[17] If God were moved by his creatures, even if he willed this for himself, he would be caused to be by another to just that extent. This violates the absolute Creator-creature distinction, rendering God partly a cause of being and partly a subject who is caused to be.[18]

Acts 17:23-29. In distinguishing the true God from all false gods, the apostle Paul declares to the Athenians that the true God is the one who made all things and does not dwell in temples made with hands, adding, "nor is he served by human hands, as though he needed anything" (Act 17:24-25).[19] There is no good that might benefit God that the creature is able to supply him. On the face of it this might strike us as incompatible with those many commands in Scripture to worship God and to serve him only. In Romans 12:1, for example, Paul exhorts believers to "present your bodies a living and holy sacrifice, acceptable to God, *which is* your spiritual service of worship" (NASB). So how can he say in Acts 17:25 that God is not *served* by human hands? His point appears to be that in our acts of service and worship God is not being *treated* or *operated on* by us.[20] When we glorify him he does not thereby receive glory he previously lacked. When we serve

---

[17]Perhaps one might point to the physician who performs an operation on himself and is thus at once both agent and patient. He can even make himself to feel pain or pleasure and thus generate new passions within himself. But such a composite being would still be partially caused to be, in the physician's case one part acting on and causing the actuality of health in another part. Precisely considered, that which receives the operation is really distinct from that which gives the operation. A being who is *a se* cannot be composed of really distinct parts (most basically of act and passive potency) since then it would depend on components of being more basic than itself in order to be all that it is. See the discussions below on pure actuality and divine simplicity.

[18]This would also hold if God moved himself to new states of being, even without the instrumental causal agency of the creature. Karl Barth proposes just such a passible, self-caused God: "But the personal God has a heart. He can feel and be affected. He is not impassible. He cannot be moved from outside by an extraneous power. But this does not mean that He is not capable of moving Himself. No, God is moved and stirred, yet not like ourselves in powerlessness, but in His own free power, in His innermost being: moved and touched by Himself." *Church Dogmatics* 2/1, trans. T. H. L. Parker et al. (Edinburgh: T&T Clark, 1957), 370 [§30.2]. Such a self-actualized God could not be simple or purely actual.

[19]The word translated "served" is from the Greek term *therapeuō*, from which we get our English terms *therapy* and *therapeutic*. It is a medical term that means to heal, to restore, to treat, or to minister. In religious contexts it can mean to worship or to serve.

[20]In Romans 12:1 Paul uses a form of the word *latreia*, which carries a strong sense of cultic or religious service. Unlike *therapeuō*, this term does not seem to carry the sense of actualizing through operation.

him through acts of love and good deeds we do not accommodate or improve him in any respect. We neither add to his blessedness nor deprive him of it. Our acts of worship are like holding a mirror to the sun; the sun's light is broadcast and shown forth by this action, but the sun itself is not made a little brighter as a result. None of our Godward activity entails that God receives the effects of our actions in the sense of being altered or changed by them.[21] It is, rather, the false gods of the nations who are helped to receive their forms of being by the actions of humans on them.

The true God is the absolute source of being, not the one who receives being from the creature. Paul raises his argument to an existential crescendo in Acts 17:28: "In him we live and move and have our being." But the inverse is not so. God is truly God precisely because, unlike the (imagined) gods of Paul's pagan interlocutors, he does not live, move, or have his being in and through the creature. If he were to derive any aspect of his life or existence from the creature, then the apostle's strong contrast between God the creator, on the one hand, and the created gods of the Athenians, on the other, would be dissolved. There is nothing in the creature—no life, breath, activity, or spark of being—that is not wholly from and through God. Moreover, in giving such things to creatures, God does not thereby divest himself of them (see Job 41:11). So the creature has no form of being by which he or she may replenish or add to God.

The error of the Athenians is that they worship beings "made by human design and skill" (Acts 17:29 NIV). The gods of Greek mythology were notorious for their passionate conflicts and dalliances with humans (and with each other). Humans wielded notable causal influence over them. In

---

[21]Some might object to this claim by pointing to petitionary prayer as an act of worship by which creatures move God. In keeping with Rom 11:36 and Acts 17:25, 28, the impassibilist maintains that prayer itself is a gift from God to his people. Thomas states, "As to its efficacy in impetrating [i.e. obtaining by entreaty], prayer derives this from the grace of God to Whom we pray, and Who instigates us to pray" (*Summa theologiae* IIa-IIae.83.15). Brian Shanley explains the role prayer plays in God's providential plan: "Prayer is efficacious not because it changes God, but because it is part of the temporal causal order arranged by God to be efficacious in the realization of God's eternal plan. Prayer does not change God's will, but rather carries it out as one of the secondary causes ordained to accomplish the divine plan. God wills that some things come about as a result of or in answer to our petitions, including our salvation. Both the prayer itself and the response are a part of God's plan. God does not have to change his will in order to will a change, and God eternally ordains that some changes take place because of our prayers." *The Thomist Tradition* (Dordrecht: Springer, 2002), 206. "Our motive in praying," writes Thomas, "is not that we may change the Divine disposition, but that, by our prayers, we may obtain what God has appointed" (*Summa theologiae* IIa-IIae.83.2, ad 2).

Paul's immediate surroundings, the idols of gold, silver, and stone happen to be the nearest thing at hand to illustrate his point. The fashioning of material idols was but an extension of the belief in passionate deities who could be manipulated by humans. Unlike the gods of the pagans, the absolute Creator of all things lacks no actuality and so can receive no form of being, whether material or immaterial, from the agency of creatures who act on him. To the question of divine impassibility, it should be observed that since all passions are accidental forms of being produced in the patient by the action of a causal agent, they must be denied of God lest the manner of his being be demoted to that of an idol, just one more god among the gods, who acts on humans and is acted on in return.

Job 35:5-8. The truth of God's aseity and independence is approached in a slightly different way in Job 35:5-8. In Job 32–37 the young man Elihu decries the impertinence of Job and the misguided counsel of his three friends.[22] Job had been righteous in his own eyes and insolently demanded God hear his case and vindicate him before his critics (Job 31:1-37; 32:1). He speaks of God as if God had some obligation to him on account of his righteous conduct. He first gave to God and so now God is beholden to him. Job is not right to assert this, contends Elihu, "for God is greater than any human being" (Job 33:12 NLT).

To drive home this point, Elihu exhorts Job and his friends, saying, "Look at the heavens and see; / observe the clouds, which are higher than you" (Job 35:5). Just as the clouds are beyond the reach of our actions, so also is God. In Job 35:6-7 Elihu argues this with regard to both the evil and good humans do:

> If you have sinned, what do you accomplish against him?
>   And if your transgressions are multiplied, what do you do to him?
> If you are righteous, what do you give to him;
>   or what does he receive from your hand?[23]

---

[22]I understand Elihu's discourse in Job 32–37 to be the inspired counsel of the wise man, serving to set up Yahweh's interrogation of Job in Job 38–41. Elihu, who ought not to be confused with Job's friends, is the only major (human) speaker in the book of Job whose words are not reproved or challenged anywhere in the book.

[23]Job 35:6 uses two different Hebrew verbs for "accomplish" (*pā'al*) and "do" (*'sah*). *pā'al* means to do or to make. *'sah* also means to do or to make, yet can sometimes convey the idea of doing or making something by pressing or squeezing, as if impressing a form into a thing. It does not seem a stretch to suppose that Elihu is talking about pressing or squeezing some form

The expression "what do you accomplish against him?" (*mah–tip'al–bo*) could also be rendered, "what do you make in him?" Elihu appears plainly to be saying that due to God's exalted existence, he is not among the beings who receive the actions of others on themselves.

Our sins, be they ever so many, have no effect on God. He is not moved by them. The same goes for our righteousness. By it, God receives in himself no benediction from us, no new form of goodness.[24] Ours sins do not disturb his being or introduce new forms of painful passion in him; and our good deeds do not improve or augment his being with new forms of pleasing passion. To whatever degree God were to receive good or ill from his creatures, he would be beholden to the creature as a cause of his being to just that degree. It is more fitting to his majesty to say he receives nothing in himself from the creature. In Job 41:11 Yahweh makes this same point: "Who has first given to me, that I should repay him? Whatever is under the whole heaven is mine" (ESV). Elihu rounds out his argument by observing that one's wicked and righteous actions have their proper effects in other humans: "Your wickedness affects others like you, / and your righteousness, other human beings" (Job 35:8). It is humans who are *done unto* by the causal actions of others on them. God, like the clouds above, is not involved in such a transaction with us. For the strong impassibilist, such considerations militate against any possibility that God might experience passion.

Pure actuality. Closely associated with divine aseity and independence is the claim that God is purely actual. Steven Duby explains:

---

of affective actuality into God, even if such precise metaphysical expressions are foreign to the Hebrew way of thinking and speaking. In the case of sinful actions perpetrated on a passible subject, the form imposed might be that of anger, pain, or sorrow. The Septuagint translates the Hebrew word עָשָׂה (from עָשָׂה) with the Greek word ποιῆσαι (from ποιέω). Recall that πάσχω (to experience, to be treated) is the passive experience corresponding to ποιέω (to do, make, cause, effect, bring about), that undergoing by which a patient receives in itself the *doing* of the agent. The fact that God cannot be *done unto* by the human agent argues strongly that he lacks the principle of passive potency by which such *doing* is received. To wit, he is impassible.

[24]Elihu's double denial—that God is moved neither by human wickedness nor righteousness—appears to be a corrective of Eliphaz's earlier half-baked argument that though God is not given pleasure by human righteousness (Job 22:2-3), he is (presumably) provoked to displeasure by Job's great and endless iniquity (Job 22:4-5). It seems that Elihu reverses the order, placing the matter of iniquity before that of righteousness in order to foreground exactly the point that Eliphaz had missed in his partly-true/partly-false diagnosis.

> Divine aseity entails . . . that God is *actus purus*. If God is entirely *a se* with
> no one and nothing back of him to account for him, then he is without causal
> susceptibility—without being moved or, indeed, a capacity to be moved—and
> therefore without the root of such causal susceptibility, namely, passive
> potency. . . . Aseity inflected as independence or *primitas* thus implies that
> God is fully in act.[25]

This teaching is motivated both by Scripture and nature in their joint witness
to God as the first principle or cause of all finite being. Biblical affirmations
of God as primary cause include such statements as these: "all things come
from God" (1 Cor 11:12); God "calls into existence the things that do not
exist" (Rom 4:17); "you created all things, / and by your will they existed and
were created" (Rev 4:11); "from him and through him and to him are all
things" (Rom 11:36; cf. 1 Cor 8:6; Jn 1:3; Col 1:16; Heb 2:10). The first cause
of being could not be the first from whom all others come if he in turn
should come from some more primordial cause. For this reason, numerous
classical theists have denied that God possesses passive potency (the principle by which new actuality is received in a being), insisting instead that he
is pure act (*actus purus*) and is being itself subsisting (*ipsum esse subsistens*).

   Thomas Aquinas develops this line of reasoning in a number of ways,
perhaps the most famous of which is his argument that the first cause of all
must be an unmoved mover: "God is the First Mover, and is Himself unmoved."[26]
Despite the great deal of scorn recently heaped on this proposal—one thinks
of Clark Pinnock's quip that such a God could be nothing more than "a metaphysical iceberg and solitary Being suffering from his own completeness"[27]—
the rationale for the doctrine is both philosophically and theologically
compelling. John Wippel provides a helpful précis of Thomas's argument:

> Nothing is moved except insofar as it is in potency to that to which it is
> moved. But something moves insofar as it is in actuality, since to move is
> nothing else but to reduce something from potency to act. And something
> can be reduced from potency to act only by some being in actuality. . . . It is
> not possible for the same thing to be in act and in potency at the same time

---

[25] Steven J. Duby, *Divine Simplicity: A Dogmatic Account,* T&T Clark Studies in Systematic Theology
(New York: T&T Clark, 2016), 121.

[26] Aquinas, *Summa theologiae* Ia.3.1.

[27] Clark H. Pinnock, *Most Moved Mover: A Theology of God's Openness* (Grand Rapids: Baker Academic, 2001), 118.

and in the same respect but only in different respects. Thus what is actually hot cannot at the same time be potentially hot . . . but is at that time potentially cold. Therefore, it is not possible for something to be mover and to be moved in the same respect by one and the same motion, or for it to move itself (in this strict sense). Therefore, everything which is moved must be moved by something else.[28]

Thomas contends that the line of moved movers "cannot go on to infinity, because then there would be no first mover, and, consequently, no other mover. . . . Therefore it is necessary to arrive at a first mover, put in motion by no other."[29]

By *first mover* Thomas means the sufficient causal reason for all movement; that cause of motion without which there could not be subsequent causes of motion. Such a being could not itself be susceptible to the reception of movement from another and so must be unmovable, possessing no passive potency. This same conclusion is set forth in a striking passage in Thomas's *Disputed Questions on the Power of God*:

Now although in one and the same thing that is at one time in act, at another time in potentiality, potentiality precedes act in time but follows it in nature: yet absolutely speaking act precedes potentiality not only in nature, but also in time, since everything that is in potentiality is made actual by some being that is in act. Accordingly the being that made all things actual, and itself proceeds from no other being, must be the first actual being without any admixture of potentiality. For were it in any way in potentiality, there would be need of another previous being to make it actual.[30]

Drawing the connection from pure actuality to divine impassibility, Thomas states that, "every passion belongs to something existing in potency. But God is completely free from potency, since He is pure act. God, therefore, is solely agent, and in no way does any passion have a place in Him."[31]

---

[28]John F. Wippel, *The Metaphysical Thought of Thomas Aquinas: From Finite Being to Uncreated Being* (Washington, DC: Catholic University of America Press, 2000), 444.

[29]Aquinas, *Summa theologiae* Ia.2.3.

[30]Thomas Aquinas, *Quaestiones disputatae de potentia Dei* 7.1, in *On the Power of God*, translated by the English Dominican Fathers (Westminster, MD: The Newman Press, 1952). See the useful discussion of God's pure actuality in Peter Weigel, *Aquinas on Simplicity: An Investigation into the Foundations of His Philosophical Theology* (Bern: Peter Lang, 2008), 103-35.

[31]Thomas Aquinas, *Summa contra gentiles* I.89, in *On the Truth of the Catholic Faith*, 5 vols., translated by Anton C. Pegis et al. (Garden City, NY: Doubleday & Company, 1955).

Critics of the unmoved mover and impassibility doctrines frequently misconstrue them as meaning that God lacks vitality, dynamism, and care for his creatures. Moltmann asks, "Is he a God? Is he not rather a stone?"[32] In the critics' thinking, to be motionless, unfeeling, and dispassionate means to be lifeless, frozen, uncaring, or indifferent. And in truth, the everyday usage of terms like motionless, apathetic, and impassive does convey precisely those notions. But in leveling the charge that impassibility renders God a "metaphysical iceberg," lifeless and uncaring, the critics appear to have completely missed the meaning of the argument from pure actuality. God is not motionless and unmovable because he lacks actuality and dynamism, but because, as pure act, he could not be made to be more actual or dynamic. Unbounded pure actuality cannot be added to and thereby moved to some additional state of actuality. As pure act God is being itself, goodness itself, life itself, love itself, justice itself, and so forth. The reason these cannot be stirred up or produced in God by the action of creatures on him is not on account of some paucity of being, virtue, or life in him, but because he is all these things in a simple unbounded act of sheer existence. Thomas Weinandy rightly observes, "God is unchangeable not because he is inert or static like a rock, but for just the opposite reason. He is so dynamic, so active that no change can make him more active. He is act pure and simple."[33]

Divine simplicity. The doctrine of divine simplicity is the negative counterpart of pure actuality, the other side of the same coin. It derives from the same biblical commitment to God as the self-sufficient first principle and cause of all finite being. Divine simplicity maintains that God is without parts.[34] A part is anything in a whole that is really distinct from—and as a part, less than—the whole and without which the whole would lack some feature of its actuality. For a part to be a part it is not necessary that it be

---

[32]Moltmann, *Crucified God*, 222.

[33]Thomas G. Weinandy, *Does God Change? The Word's Becoming in the Incarnation* (Still River, MA: St. Bede's, 1985), 79.

[34]The doctrine is clearly set forth by Thomas Aquinas in *Summa theologiae* Ia.3 and *Disputed Questions on the Power of God* 7. Lengthier treatments can be found in Weigel, *Aquinas on Simplicity*; Duby, *Divine Simplicity*; and James E. Dolezal, *God Without Parts: Divine Simplicity and the Metaphysics of God's Absoluteness* (Eugene, OR: Pickwick, 2011). For a brief discussion of how multipart speech and thinking about God squares with his simplicity, see James E. Dolezal, *All That Is in God: Evangelical Theology and the Challenge of Classical Christian Theism* (Grand Rapids: Reformation Heritage Books, 2017), 43, 59-60, 67-78.

able to exist in a separated state, but only that it be less than the whole and a contributor to the whole's actuality. The being of every composite whole depends in some respect on its parts. Composite entities also depend on a source of unity that causes their parts to cohere together, that is, on an agent of composition. Classical theists deny that God is composed of parts inasmuch as a composite God would be doubly dependent for his actuality on that which is not God: on the parts themselves, and on the composer supplying unity to the parts. The underlying conviction is that nothing that is not God makes him to be. Indeed, all that is in God just is God.[35]

Divine simplicity proscribes the possibility of passions in God precisely because every passion is an accidental part of the substance in which it inheres. The substance is in passive potency to the actuality provided by the accident. It receives from the accident a new determination of being and is to that extent caused to be by the accident. But God, being *a se* and purely actual, cannot stand in passive potency to causes of his being. If God loves, is merciful, gracious, or opposes sin, it cannot be on account of a variety of really distinct accidental forms such as love, mercy, compassion, or self-vindicating justice somehow inhering in him. Those virtues that are predicated of creatures accidentally are predicated of God substantively. Divine simplicity maintains that God *just is* the love by which he loves, *just is* the kindness by which he is merciful and gracious, *just is* the perfect justice and consuming fire of holiness by which he demonstrates wrath against sin, and so forth. God's love, mercy, vindicative justice, and the like are not non-God constituents making him to be what he otherwise would not have been.

Such virtues are not passions in God because they are not states of being into which God is moved on account of some causal action befalling him. In God no process of undergoing actualizes his virtues.[36] It is a profoundly

---

[35]Stephen Charnock writes, "God is the most simple being; for that which is first in nature, having nothing beyond it, cannot by any means be thought to be compounded; for whatsoever is so, depends upon the parts whereof it is compounded, and so is not the first being: now God being infinitely simple, hath nothing in himself which is not himself, and therefore cannot will any change in himself, he being his own essence and existence." *The Existence and Attributes of God*, 2 vols. (1853; repr., Grand Rapids: Baker, 1979), 1:333.

[36]John of Damascus states that "being simple and uncompounded, and consequently, by nature unaffected and unchanging, He is by nature not subject to passion or change." *The Orthodox Faith* 1.8, in *Saint John of Damascus: Writings*, trans. Frederic H. Chase Jr., Fathers of the Church, vol. 37 (New York: Fathers of the Church, Inc., 1958).

misguided accusation to charge that impassible love, mercy, kindness, and self-vindicating justice are made less genuine or intense simply because they do not come about in God through a process of change enacted within him by the creature. Nothing could be further from the truth. In God such virtues are infinitely *more* lively and dynamic than in their passionate creaturely counterparts inasmuch as they are nothing but the unbounded fullness of God's act of being itself.

GOOD NEWS OF GOD'S IMPASSIBLE LOVE

Creatures can imitate God by their acts of love toward one another. But this imitation necessarily remains restricted to the creaturely modalities of finitude and becoming. For us love will always remain an acquired accidental state, habit, or virtue. But God's love is not an acquired form he comes to possess in addition to being God. Rather, God's love is identical with his being: "God is love" (1 Jn 4:8). Given its commitment to God's aseity and independence, pure actuality, and simplicity, strong impassibility is uniquely positioned to account for the true freedom and unboundedness of God's love. All instances of passionate love are finite states of caused actuality visited on the subject. This does not mean such love cannot be genuine or dynamic, but only that it is finite, mutable, and beholden to a cause—lacking the absolute freedom and gratuity that uniquely characterizes the love of God for the creature.

A purely beneficent love. On the passibilist account, divine creation and love cannot be ultimately altruistic or gratuitous inasmuch as a passible God is seeking some new good for himself in his acts of creation and love. Consider Jürgen Moltmann's argument. He insists that "the lack of any creative movement would mean an imperfection in the Absolute."[37] In creating, God is seeking a perfection for himself he would otherwise lack. Moreover, in redeeming creatures God is in fact seeking deliverance for himself. Moltmann writes:

> The creation of the world and human beings for freedom and fellowship is always bound up with the process of God's deliverance from the sufferings of his love. His love, which liberates, delivers and redeems through suffering,

---

[37]Moltmann, *Trinity and the Kingdom*, 45.

wants to reach its fulfillment in the love that is bliss. But love only finds bliss
when it finds its beloved, liberates them, and has them eternally at his side.
For that reason and in this sense the deliverance or redemption of the world
is bound up with the self-deliverance of God from his sufferings. In this sense,
not only does God suffer with and for the world; liberated men and women
suffer with God and for him.[38]

For Moltmann, God lacks love's fulfilling bliss and therefore goes outside
himself in order to obtain it from and through the creature.

All passionate love is a movement of the lover toward some perceived
good in the thing loved. It is a volitional inclination toward, and a reaching
out for, the good presented to it, and is called forth into actuality by that
good.[39] If the love by which God created the world were a passionate love,
then his creation would not be an act of pure generosity. It would be caused
by some good presented to him by the world. If his saving love for the sinner
were a passionate love, then salvation would not be all of grace. It would be
caused to a significant degree by some goodness in the sinner, compelling
God to reach out and seek him or her. The gospel of God's free grace can
be consistently maintained only to the extent that his love for the sinner is
without passion.

The prophecy of Hosea speaks a great deal about love and lovers, dis-
closing a sordid affair in which God showers the people of Israel with gifts
of love, and yet the people, like lustful harlots, run after other gods, for-
getting Yahweh, their husband and provider. There is nothing about the
people that appears good or lovely; every description of their conduct
renders them utterly repulsive. Yet, more outstanding than the ugliness of
the people is the love God demonstrates and promises for them. Despite
her profound iniquity, God continues to provide for Israel and to declare
his purpose to draw her back to himself in kindness. The apogee of this
staggering generosity appears in the words of Hosea 14:4: "I will heal their

---

[38]Moltmann, *Trinity and the Kingdom*, 60. How is Moltmann's confirmation that God seeks fulfillment from his creatures not a contradiction of his assertion that God suffers out of the fullness
of his being?

[39]Weinandy observes that passion "denotes a change in that the knowledge of a known good motivates
and arouses the will to desire the good known and loved, and to seek ways to obtain the good." He
adds, "There is no passion in God because, being pure act, there is no need for arousal to the good and
desire for the good. Thus God loves himself and all things in himself in the one act which he himself
is because in the one act he knows and wills himself as pure goodness" (*Does God Change?*, 79).

disloyalty; / I will love them freely, / for my anger has turned from them."
What ultimately makes this love free is that it is unmotivated by the people
themselves. It is not some goodness in them that moves God to love them so.

Ephesians 2 also spotlights the pure gratuity of God's love for us. We
read in Ephesians 2:4 of God's "great love with which he loved us" even
when we were dead in our trespasses and sins, when we were utterly lacking
in moral goodness. In Ephesians 2:8 we are told how Christians come to be
the recipients of this great love: "For by grace you have been saved through
faith, and this is not your own doing; it is the gift of God." But if God's
great love by which he poured out his grace on us were a passionate love,
then his saving grace would in fact turn out to be our "own doing" (*ex humōn*:
of you or *from you*) inasmuch as we would be the agents by which this love is
produced in God.[40] Suffice it to say, God's saving love is made unfree and
is deprived of its truly gracious character to whatever extent the creature is
the cause of it, that is, to the extent it is a passionate love.

Impassibility ensures that God's love for the creature is not an acquisitive
love that seeks goodness *from* the creature, but rather it is a creative love that
bestows goodness *on* the creature. Thomas Aquinas explains:

> God loves all existing things. For all existing things, in so far as they exist, are
> good, since the existence of a thing is itself a good; and likewise, whatever
> perfection it possesses. Now ... God's will is the cause of all things. It must
> needs be, therefore, that a thing has existence, or any kind of good, only in-
> asmuch as it is willed by God. To every existing thing, then, God wills some
> good. Hence, since to love anything is nothing else than to will good to that
> thing, it is manifest that God loves everything that exists. Yet not as we love.
> Because since our will is not the cause of the goodness of things, but is moved
> by it as by its object, our love, whereby we will good to anything, is not the
> cause of its goodness; but conversely its goodness, whether real or imaginary,
> calls forth our love, by which we will that it should preserve the good it has,
> and receive besides the good it has not, and to this end we direct our actions:
> whereas the love of God infuses and creates goodness.[41]

---

[40]When Paul says God's saving grace is not "of yourselves," he rules out not only our works as sources
of our salvation (moving God to save us), but also our depraved natures (see Eph 2:3).

[41]Aquinas, *Summa theologiae* Ia.20.2. See the discussion in Michael J. Dodds, *The Unchanging God
of Love: Thomas Aquinas and Contemporary Theology on Divine Immutability*, 2nd ed. (Washington,
DC: Catholic University of America Press, 2008), 204-13.

To put the matter plainly, impassible love causes the creature's good to be, while passible love is caused to be by some good in the creature. These alternatives are mutually exclusive: either God's love for the creature actualizes the creature's good or the creature's good actualizes God's love for the creature. The good news of God's impassible saving love is that it freely bestows goodness and loveliness on the morally defiled and unlovely.

A jealous and diversely manifested love. Exodus 34:14 states, "The LORD, whose name is Jealous, is a jealous God." Jealousy is the zeal that accompanies all acts of intense love. Thomas observes that "intense love seeks to remove everything that opposes it."[42] Insomuch as it is God's nature to love his own goodness, it is also his nature to resist and remove all that opposes his goodness. Among moral creatures he does this either through redemption or through judgment, and in fact throughout Holy Scripture we find that redemption and judgment are inseparable. There is only salvation where God has first removed the powers hostile to the sinner. We ought not to think of God's hostility to sin as though it were love's evil twin, a second and really distinct form of being sitting awkwardly in him alongside his love and joy. His perfect abhorrence of sin, rather, is nothing but his love for his own goodness considered as his jealous and self-vindicating justice.

When shown forth in God's providential dealings with moral creatures, his love can appear as either mercy or wrath, either grace or self-vindicating jealousy. Toward the objects of God's saving love, it appears as merciful redemption. These are the "objects of mercy" (Rom 9:23) who gratefully confess, "God has destined us not for wrath but for obtaining salvation through our Lord Jesus Christ" (1 Thess 5:9). Toward those sinners to whom he deems not to apply redemptive grace, his jealous love appears as wrath and anger. They are "objects of wrath that are made for destruction" (Rom 9:22) on whom God fixes his eyes "for harm and not for good" (Amos 9:4). The same divine love that bestows salvation on some sinners pours forth condemnation on others.[43]

---

[42]Aquinas, *Summa theologiae* Ia-IIae.28.4.

[43]Thomas holds that God wills the evil of punishment insomuch as punishment is but the "evil" corollary of his love for the good to which evil parasitically clings: "The evil . . . of punishment, He does will, by willing the good to which such evils are attached. Thus in willing justice He wills punishment" (*Summa theologiae* Ia.19.9).

This brings us finally to the question of whether purely actual love must be manifested in and on all creatures in exactly the same manner. Pure act does not admit of degrees or variation. Yet the manifestation of God's purely actual love, seen in the good he gives to creatures, does not seem to touch every creature in precisely the same way. Among fallen humans, it touches some in the form of mercy and grace and others in the form of wrath and judgment. What are we to make of this diversity?

First, we should observe that the good God wills for his creatures is a created similitude of his essential goodness and not his essence itself. "Therefore," as Thomas notes, "there is no reason why it may not vary in degree."[44] Second, God need not will every good to every creature. He can love a person as existing, existence being the most fundamental good conferred on creatures, but abhor the same person as sinful, insomuch as sin is the absence of good where it ought to be.[45] Scripture witnesses to the bounty of goods God gives to the righteous and wicked alike (Mt 5:45; Acts 14:17) without suggesting that every possible good is equally distributed to all (Ps 17:13-15; 73:3; Mal 1:2-3). Third, God's love, being impassible, is neither caused by the creature nor owed to it. This means God is utterly free in discriminating among his creatures with regard to the portion of good he chooses to give each one. The reason for this unequal distribution does not lie in the creatures to whom good is given, but in God who is free to give what is his own. In the natural world at large this is evinced in the greater dignity he grants to some things over others—for example, to living beings over nonliving, sensible beings over merely vegetative, rational beings over all nonrational. In the moral realm this is shown in the mercy given to some sinners but withheld from others (see Rom 9:13-24).

In God, the divine act of love is identical with his pure and simple act of existence. It therefore admits of no greater or lesser intensity. And in this respect we should say God loves all his creatures with the exact same love. But with regard to the manifestation of that love there is diversity and disproportionality in the goods given to creatures, grounded in God's free will to distribute good as he pleases. From this vantage point we must say God loves some more than others.[46]

---

[44]Aquinas, *Summa theologiae* Ia.20.3, ad 2.
[45]See Aquinas, *Summa theologiae* Ia.20.2, ad 4.
[46]See Aquinas, *Summa theologiae* Ia.20.3.

REVEALING IMPASSIBLE LOVE
UNDER THE FORM OF THE PASSIBLE

Having considered the basic motivations and logic of the impassibility doctrine, we must finally consider how to approach the passages of Scripture that portray God as undergoing passion and how it is that the impassible Son of God suffers. In both the Bible and in the Son's suffering, God discloses his impassible love and self-affirming justice under the form of the passible.

Manifesting the infinite in finite structures. Impassible love, being identical with God's pure and unbounded act of existence, cannot be comprehended by the human mind in a one-to-one fashion. The finite cannot contain the infinite. This does not mean God's love and justice cannot be truly known by humans, but only that they cannot be comprehended in that unparalleled manner in which they are in God. In order to make known to us the truth of his unbounded being, God condescends to refract and repackage that truth into approachable structures of finitude. This accommodation is properly located in the order of divine revelation and providence among creatures, and not in the being of God himself.

We see something of this in the words of Solomon in 1 Kings 8:27 at the dedication of the temple: "But will God indeed dwell on the earth? Even heaven and the highest heaven cannot contain you, much less this house that I have built!" Solomon is acutely aware of the profound incommensurability between the manner of God's being and the manner in which he discloses himself and draws near to the creature. While God condescends to fill finite human structures with manifestations of his presence and truth, we ought not to think he has thereby been captured in a one-to-one way in these finite forms. Touching the matter of biblical revelation, we should bear in mind that Scripture's language and manner of speaking about God, like Solomon's temple, is a finite human structure in and through which God deigns to manifest himself to us. But it is not a structure that is equal to his manner of being.[47]

---

[47]All biblical God-talk is analogical in the sense that it takes its point of departure from God's effects. Bavinck observes, "We have no knowledge of God other than that from his revelation in the creaturely world. . . . Of God we have no direct but only an indirect kind of knowledge, a concept derived from the creaturely world" (*Reformed Dogmatics*, 2:130). This does not mean all biblical God-talk is metaphorical. Analogical and accommodated revelation does not rule out the

That said, the impassibilist regards the many biblical ascriptions of passion to God to be accommodated ways of speaking by which God discloses his love and justice in ordinary forms of humans experience, like houses which truly manifest divine presence and yet do not properly correspond to God's actual manner of existence. Most readers of the Bible tend to instinctively do this with those passages that attribute to God body parts and actions unique to material beings. With few exceptions, modern exegetes, even many who reject divine impassibility, consistently interpret such language to be a metaphorical manner of speaking that does not actually match the precise manner of God's existence and activity. They do this even though there are far more passages that speak of God as material than speak of him as immaterial. The conviction that corporeity is proper only to creatures dictates that every biblical attribution of corporeity to God be regarded as nonliteral. And if that underlying conviction is biblically funded and theologically sound, then so are the interpretive judgments that flow from it.

The impassibilist does effectively the same thing with respect to Scripture's depictions of change in God. As all corporeal language is deemed anthropomorphic (or zoomorphic, or geomorphic) by the immaterialist, so all passion language is deemed anthropopathic by the impassibilist. The impassibilist's controlling theological principle is that being caused to be is proper only to creatures and therefore must be altogether denied of God. Consider, for instance, Genesis 6:6: "And the LORD was sorry that he had made humankind on the earth, and it grieved him to his heart." The standard impassibilist conclusion is that this text reveals God's just opposition to sin, but under a form of modality proper only to changeable creatures. John Calvin writes, "The repentance which is here ascribed to God does not properly belong to him, but has reference to our understanding of him. . . . This figure, which represents God as transferring to himself what is peculiar to human nature, is called *anthropopatheia*."[48] Matthew Henry says God

---

possibility of distinguishing between proper and improper predication about God. See the important discussion in Gregory P. Rocca, *Speaking the Incomprehensible God: Thomas Aquinas on the Interplay of Positive and Negative Theology* (Washington, DC: Catholic University of America Press, 2004), 291-333.

[48]John Calvin, *Commentaries on the First Book of Moses Called Genesis*, trans. John King (Grand Rapids: Eerdmans, 1948), 1:248-49.

speaks here "after the manner of men" and that this language "does not imply any passion or uneasiness in God." It discloses, in accommodated fashion, God's "just and holy displeasure against sin and sinners."[49] John Gill concurs: "This is speaking by anthropopathy, after the manner of men, because God determined to do, and did something similar to men, when they repent of anything." God's grief of heart is to be regarded as anthropopathic language, "for God is a simple Being, uncompounded, and not subject to any passions and affections."[50] John Wesley writes in the same vein: "These are expressions after the manner of men, and must be understood so as not to reflect upon God's immutability or felicity. It doth not speak any passion or uneasiness in God."[51]

If the doctrines of aseity and independence, pure actuality, and simplicity are funded by divine revelation and are theologically sound, then so are the interpretive judgments that necessarily flow from these doctrines. This interpretation does not in any way undermine the truth about God's love or holy opposition to sin, but only claims that these perfections are not made actual in God by the action of the creature on him. Human actions are simply the occasions on which God variously manifests his unchanging love and justice, appearing to us under the forms of mercy or wrath accordingly.

It matters not how many passion texts there may be. In order to falsify divine impassibility, the critic must convincingly show that its principles lack funding from divine revelation and are therefore either unsound or unmotivated. The doctrine could also be undermined if it could be shown that its supposed benefits could be had in some other way that would allow for passions in God. Absent such convincing alternatives, the impassibilist understandably continues to insist that all biblical attribution of passion to God is nonliteral.

Christ's passion. Perhaps some might imagine that the suffering of the divine Son on the cross is sufficient to deflate the impassibility doctrine. Impassibilists do not find this argument compelling inasmuch as they locate Christ's suffering properly in his humanity and not his divinity. After

---

[49]Matthew Henry, *Commentary on the Whole Bible:* Vol. 1, *Genesis to Deuteronomy* (London: Fleming H. Revell, n.d.), 53.
[50]John Gill, *Gill's Commentaries* (Grand Rapids: Baker, 1980), 1:38.
[51]John Wesley, *Explanatory Notes upon the Old Testament* (Bristol: William Pine, 1765), 1:31.

affirming his robust commitment to divine impassibility, James Arminius concludes, "Therefore, Christ has not suffered according to the Essence of his Deity."[52] This standard impassibilist reasoning is in keeping with the Chalcedonian Formula that confesses the incarnate Son "in two natures, inconfusedly, unchangeably, indivisibly, inseparably." What is proper to his humanity does not wash over into his divinity, or vice versa.

This does not mean the passions of the Son in his humanity do not reveal to us the love and justice of God. We should think of Christ's passions of suffering love (Mt 23:37; Jn 11:32-35; 15:13) and righteous anger (Mk 3:5; Jn 2:13-17; Rev 6:16) as disclosures of God's impassible love and perfect justice under the form of the finite, the form of the passible. Jesus' passionate love and anger, being proper to his human nature, are not modally equivalent to his divine love and justice. Nevertheless, they do serve as suitable and illuminating refractions or translations, so to speak, of those impassible virtues of his divinity. The nonliteral, anthropopathic language by which Scripture speaks of God comes to literal expression in the passions of God the Son incarnate. God *as divine* does not literally undergo affliction with his people in his act of saving them (see Is 63:7-9), but the Son of God *as human* does undergo such affliction on behalf of the people he saves (Is 53; 1 Pet 2:24). Far from posing a problem for divine impassibility, the passions of Christ are but the most sublime manifestations of God's impassible love and justice, being brilliantly shown forth within the structure of the Son's finite and passible human nature.[53]

CONCLUSION

The dynamic stillness of impassible love and impassible jealousy is infinitely more vital and energetic than the most fervent instances of passionate love and jealousy imaginable. As impassible, God could not possibly be more loving, caring, or opposed to sin than he is from all eternity. God's passionless love and jealousy are nothing but God himself subsisting as pure

---

[52]James Arminius, *The Works of James Arminius*, trans. James Nichols (Grand Rapids: Baker, 1986), 2:117. For a careful account of Christ's human passions, see Paul Gondreau, *The Passions of Christ's Soul in the Theology of St. Thomas Aquinas* (Münster: Aschendorff Verlag, 2002).

[53]This is not to suggest that the union of God the Son with his human nature is of the same sort as God's presence in his temple. The former is a hypostatic union, entirely unique, whereas the latter is an indwelling of grace.

act, whereas their passionate counterparts within creatures are instances of actualized finitude. The distance between these two is nothing less than the distance between being and becoming, between God and all that comes to be through dependence on him.

A Qualified Impassibility Response

DANIEL CASTELO

In my estimation, Dolezal's chapter is a solid case for divine impassibility. A number of claims that one would expect in such a chapter are presented therein, making it a helpful survey piece for readers. He cites one of the most important contemporary advocates of divine impassibility (Thomas Weinandy) as well as explores statements and figures from the Christian heritage. It is interesting to note (as he does) just how widely the notion of divine impassibility has been affirmed. One may have different theories as to why that is, but its prevalence up to the modern era is indisputable.

Dolezal is right to claim that impassibility's appeal has traditionally been to "safeguard God's fullness and perfection of being." In other words, at stake with impassibility is the promotion of an account of the Christian God that highlights God's greatness and God's worship-worthiness in a way that recognizes the difference between God and the world. Impassibility assumes many things, but one is that God is unique, self-sufficient, and beyond the limits and parameters of existence as we humans understand and experience it. The appeal of this vision rests on the assumption that contingency, dependency, and limitation are not fitting for a god that is worship worthy. Although Dolezal could have done more with the biblical materials (as could have I in my own chapter), there is a strand of biblical materials that highlights these points significantly, and frankly, often this witness does not make the rounds in terms of Christian teaching and emphasis.

As advocating for a qualified impassibilist position, I am on the same side of the divide as Dolezal, although he does take on matters differently than I do. For instance, although he makes some allusions to the Creator-creation divide and suggests the importance of keeping it intact, he could have done more with the doctrine of creation for the sake of orienting the reader. From my end, I am inclined to think that this move bears repeating as much as is allowable simply because of how crucial it is for impassibility's theological credibility. For those who say that impassibility is a heretical import, I think the most significant doctrinal counterpoint has to be a doctrine of creation with the Creator-creation distinction front and center. Furthermore, Dolezal does not explore the apophatic role impassibility can play in doctrinal speech, which perhaps is more indicative of a qualified rather than a strong approach to impassibility since it relates more to the function of the notion than its definition. Having said that, I do think that the apophatic role is quite important to highlight especially as spaces for linguistic and conceptual unsettling are needed in order to make divine impassibility viable in the contemporary situation.

My one strong reservation with Dolezal's chapter is that I worry about how appealing it can be to those who are not already convinced of its metaphysical architecture. And I register this worry because most of the main arguments he makes require a commitment to a particular metaphysical and conceptual framework that is both intricate and difficult to sustain amid other alternatives more prevalent today. Dolezal reflects this commitment early on when he remarks, "Talk about God's passibility or impassibility is, at bottom, talk about divine actuality." In some ways, I understand what Dolezal is after. Actuality, alongside simplicity and aseity, suggests a metaphysical landscape that by its very construal has as its boogeymen contingency, dependency, change, potential, passivity, and the like. I agree that at some level these boogeymen need to be resisted because, if they are not, the anthropomorphization of Christian God-talk can be taken too far (as when it is not even recognized as a possibility or a threat). But if the anthropomorphization of Christian God-talk is a worry that is vigilantly resisted, I wonder if the language of change, contingency, causation, and the like (specifically as narrated in Scripture) can nevertheless be allowed in some fashion beyond Dolezal's metaphysical framework to good, faith-building effect.

Let me put the matter another way. Dolezal's presentation works out of an assumption that we can press intellectually and conceptually beyond and behind our realities with categories from our realities to secure something over and against them for the sake of making sense of the Scriptural witness of who God is. For people who are not already convinced of this assumption, it is very difficult to make a case for it in our postcritical age, which would ask if that very assumption betrays a Western sensibility tied to various power-laden operational beliefs that "we" can make such claims in such absolutist ways (e.g., "God *is* pure actuality" or "God *is* the perfection of being"). I sympathize with those who would come away from Dolezal's chapter wondering if it was ultimately about the intricacies of a particular conceptual apparatus, given the attention required to define and elaborate that apparatus for the eventual payoff of it having some connection with the Scriptural witness. Also, some may come away from this presentation thinking that creation is disparaged in the effort to elevate the Creator and that the dynamic is not some kind of lively interface. After all, the biblical writers cast the Creator and creation in dynamic, interactive ways. Again, we all have to come clean with the conceptual commitments we bring to the Bible because we all have them. But I am convinced that one conceptual apparatus cannot account for all of the intricacies, claims, and characteristics Scripture brings regarding the God of our common worship. I believe we have to start with this witness, full as it is with its many uplifting *and* troublesome qualities, and then move to account for it in terms of various conceptual possibilities, which at the end of the day, will be tentative and revisable. Dolezal's conceptual apparatus has a respectable pedigree, and it also accounts for some very important matters that ultimately aim to safe-guard God's worship-worthiness. Oftentimes, this apparatus is ill-understood, but it has something to teach us in the present given that it accounts for things neglected in other metaphysical systems. These many factors con-tribute to why I allow myself to be considered as advocating "qualified im-passibility." And yet, I would say this apparatus is an option among many other conceptual options, and just as it accounts for some features of the Scriptural witness well, other options may account for other features well too. For me (this sensibility most likely stems from my multiracial/multiethnic background), the goal is not to be a devotee to a particular conceptual apparatus or school; the goal, rather, is to learn from multiple schools or approaches so that what needs to be professed or announced makes its way into the public square. For me, the metaphysical commitments undergirding Dolezal's chapter sound a bit too pronounced to the point of being distracting to some significant claims and concerns, including the narration of the divine character within history, in terms of Christology (which unfortunately receives little treatment until the end) and pneumatology (which is absent from the chapter altogether, from what I recall).

A Qualified Passibility Response

JOHN C. PECKHAM

I appreciate how clearly James E. Dolezal lays out his position. Much of Dolezal's account hinges on his claim that his view is the "classical doctrine" with "wide ecumenical backing." Yet there is considerable disagreement over how to interpret Christian tradition in this regard. Dolezal's claims that "historically, there is no recognized 'weak' variant of the impassibility doctrine" and "no such cogent alternative is genuinely possible" are sure to be contested by some. Whatever one makes of such disputed claims, I appreciate that Dolezal recognizes that "broad historical support by no means fixes the truth of the doctrine."

One wonders, then, how much weight Dolezal's scholastic metaphysical framework should carry. Is it biblically warranted, and should Scripture be allowed, at least in principle, to reform it? Dolezal offers no texts or passages that indicate divine impassibility but appeals to other claims to ground divine impassibility and, to his credit, attempts to offer biblical support for those claims. However, in my view, his attempts are largely unpersuasive.

While I agree that Romans 11:35-36 indicates that God is indebted to no one (for his existence, essential nature, or otherwise), I do not see how this passage indicates that God, in Dolezal's words, "exists independently of all causal influence from his creatures." Further, while God is undoubtedly the "primary cause" (1 Cor 11:12; Rom 4:17; Rev 4:11; Rom 11:36), as far as I can see, none of the texts Dolezal cites evince pure actuality. Moreover, I am not confident that we should take Elihu's speech (Job 35:3-8) as divinely sanctioned and, even if so, I'm not sure it entails Dolezal's view.

With regard to Acts 17:23-29, I agree that Acts 17:25 teaches that God is self-sufficient in the sense that he *needs* nothing, but I take this text to mean that God is not "served" in any way that entails that God needs anything. Dolezal's view, however, requires that even the kinds of service that God commands of humans make no difference to God. God, then, cannot actually be pleased or displeased by humans.

Scripture repeatedly teaches just the opposite. God delights in loving-kindness, justice, and righteousness (Jer 9:24). God "takes pleasure in those who fear him" (Ps 147:11) and, while "the sacrifice of the wicked is an abomination to the LORD," the "prayer of the upright is his delight" (Prov 15:8). Christians are to walk in a manner "worthy of the Lord, fully pleasing [*areskeia*] to him" (Col 1:10; cf. Col 3:20; Heb 11:5). In these and many other texts, Scripture directly contradicts the view that God cannot be pleased by creatures.

Further, whereas Dolezal claims that human sins "have no effect on God" and "do not disturb his being or introduce new forms of painful passion in him," (23)[1] text after text portrays God as being displeased, grieved, pained, and provoked to anger and passion (see, e.g., Gen 6:6-7; Deut 9:7; 32:21; Ps 78:40-41; cf. 1 Cor 10:5). Dolezal later affirms "God's hostility to sin" but such "hostility" (on his account) cannot actually be provoked by sin. This is difficult to square with the biblical data, to say the least.

In my view, the texts Dolezal employs are severely underdetermined relative to the metaphysical claims he makes over against divine passibility. Further, I believe other texts contradict those claims.[2] Notably, Dolezal elsewhere recognizes, "many passages of the Bible" do indeed "speak of God as undergoing affective changes."[3]

The situation relative to biblical support, then, is this: we have no passages that indicate divine impassibility and we have an abundance of passages that "speak of God as undergoing affective changes." Dolezal maintains, however,

---

[1]Page numbers in parentheses represent quoted material found elsewhere in this book.
[2]See John C. Peckham, *The Love of God: A Canonical Model* (Downers Grove, IL: IVP Academic, 2015), 147-89, 263-69.
[3]James E. Dolezal, "Still Impassible: Confessing God Without Passions," *Journal of the Institute of Reformed Baptist Studies* 1 (2014): 134.

that such passages should not be understood as accurately portraying God as he actually is because biblical language is accommodative to human understanding (the accommodative language rationale) and God is impassible (the impassibility rationale). However, for the reasons briefly explained in my chapter, I do not think these rationales suffice to overturn the exegetical upshot of Scripture.

Here, Dolezal's argument for divine impassibility is only as strong as the other metaphysical claims from which he argues, which not only appear to lack sufficient biblical support but are the subject of considerable disagreement among Christian theists. In this regard, Dolezal maintains that *if* God is pure actuality, simple (in the strong sense Dolezal defines), *a se* and self-sufficient in the way Dolezal maintains, timeless (such that God is without temporal succession), and strongly immutable, then God *must be* strongly impassible. However, one might argue in reverse: if God is passible in the sense that he is affected by and responsive to creatures, as Scripture portrays, then God cannot be pure actuality, simple (in the strong sense Dolezal defines), *a se* and self-sufficient in the way Dolezal maintains, timeless, or strongly immutable.

To be clear, alongside qualified divine passibility, I affirm divine aseity and self-sufficiency, understood to mean that God's existence and essential nature are not dependent on or derived from anything outside of himself.[4] God's existence is eternal, uncaused, and entirely independent of the world, which God freely created *ex nihilo*. Although God is *voluntarily* passible in relation to the world, God's essential nature is entirely independent and not contingent on anything else.

This coheres with a qualified, yet robust, conception of divine immutability wherein God's essential nature and character do not change but God can and does enter into *real* relationship with creatures and changes (relationally) accordingly. Such a view allows one to consistently affirm *both* the biblical testimony that God does not change with respect to his essential nature and character (cf. Mal 3:6) *and* the biblical testimony that God does actually experience (analogically) the kinds of relational "changes" Scripture regularly attributes to God (e.g., with regard to accidental properties such

---

[4]See R. T. Mullins, *The End of the Timeless God* (New York: Oxford University Press, 2016), 139, 62–63.

basic qualified pass. position + motivation

as being pleased or angered by creaturely actions). So understood, qualified divine passibility poses no threat to the aseity, self-sufficiency, or immutability of God's essential being.

Dolezal also argues from a conception of divine love as impassible. Yet does Scripture actually support this conception of divine love? Dolezal's concept of divine love excludes any *real* relation between God and creatures. Scripture, on the other hand, explicitly and consistently portrays God as voluntarily involved in *real*, reciprocal (but asymmetrical) love relationship with creatures (Hos 14:4).[5] Whereas Dolezal claims that God's love, joy, mercy, and jealousy are not affected by humans *at all*, Scripture repeatedly and explicitly depicts aspects of God's love, joy, mercy, and jealousy as responsive to creatures and thus possible (see, e.g., Ex 20:6; Deut 7:12-13; 1 Kings 14:22; Is 55:7; 62:4; Jer 16:5; Hos 11:8-9; Zeph 3:17; Lk 1:50; Jn 14:23; cf. Jas 2:13).

Whereas Dolezal contends that, were God to take pleasure in love relationships with creatures, the generosity of love would be undermined, Scripture repeatedly affirms that God may be pleased and displeased by creatures. Yet this entails no inadequacy in God, as if God *needs* to receive some value from creatures (contra Moltmann) or can be in any way improved.

God is the ultimate source of all value and love: "We love because he first loved us" (1 Jn 4:19). Humans have nothing to offer that has not been given to us (1 Cor 4:7) or that is unsoiled by sin (Is 64:6). Yet even as a human father can be deeply moved and pleased when his young child offers him a gift that is otherwise worthless (and bought with his own money), through faith in Jesus Christ, humans may "offer spiritual sacrifices acceptable to God" (1 Pet 2:5) and thus be "pleasing in his sight" (Heb 13:21). As such, God's love and favor is always unmerited by humans. Here God taking pleasure in human offerings (mediated by Christ) would no more make humans the cause of God's *essential* being than taking pleasure in a gift from my eight-year-old son would make him the cause of my *essential* being.

Yet Dolezal maintains, "All passionate love is a movement of the lover toward some perceived good in the thing loved." However, on the contrary, Scripture repeatedly portrays God as moved to compassionate love (e.g.,

---

[5]See Peckham, *Love of God*.

Jer 31:20; Hos 11:8; cf. Mt 20:34) and pity (Judg 2:18) by the plight and neediness of humanity. God's salvation of sinners can be "all of grace" and utterly unselfish while, at the same time, it is true that, "for the sake of the joy that was set before him," Christ "endured the cross" (Heb 12:2).

In these and many other ways, Scripture teaches that God's love is responsive and that God is capable of being affected by creatures and thus passible in relation to the world, contra strong impassibility.

A Strong Passibility Response

THOMAS JAY OORD

James E. Dolezal's essay on strong impassibility nicely defends what I regard as half of what we ought to say about God. I think we should affirm the impassibility and immutability of God's *nature*. But Dolezal rejects good arguments and biblical support for the passibility and mutability of God's *experience*. As I see it, Dolezal gets divine passibility half right and half wrong.

Dolezal recognizes that his position strikes many, as he puts it, as "absurd and maybe even repugnant" (13). He knows there is ample biblical support for God's relationality. But Dolezal appeals mainly to leading thinkers of yesteryear and the ancient metaphysics they embraced. Those on the list of yesteryear thinkers are not consistently in favor of his view, however. John Wesley's theology, for instance, supports both impassibility and passibility. Christian history is less consistent on the meaning of divine impassibility than what some theologians claim.

The failure to distinguish between God's nature and God's experience lead Dolezal to worry about God depending on creatures. God cannot be "the absolute Creator on whom all creatures ultimately depend," says Dolezal, "if it turns out that he himself depends on his creatures, or on any other cause, for some aspect of his being" (14).

If Dolezal embraces the distinction between God's nature and experience, however, he could say the states of God's experience (God's "being," in his language) depend partly on creatures, while God's nature does not. God is independent in one sense and dependent in another.

The failure to distinguish between God's nature and experience also becomes evident in Dolezal's words about love. He thinks, for instance, we must choose between saying "God loves his creatures with an unbounded act of free and uncaused love, or he loves them with a finite, caused, and mutable love" (15).

I believe we should say God's loving nature is the uncaused source of God loving creatures. But the experiential way God loves moment by moment is partially caused by God's relations with creatures. In other words, God's nature leads God to love creatures necessarily, while God freely chooses how to express this love.

Dolezal presents a theology based almost entirely on disanalogies between the Creator and creatures. For instance, he speaks of God's love, joy, mercy, and jealousy as entirely disanalogous to creaturely love, joy, mercy, and jealousy. In God these expressions are not relational, in the sense of giving and receiving. In creatures, they are relational. "God himself is of himself," Dolezal argues in support of disanalogy, "though not in the same way creatures are" (18). In my view, Dolezal's views based on disanalogies are far more "nonsensical" than Moltmann's.

When it comes to divine aseity and simplicity, Dolezal also gets the issues half right. He says God is, in all respects, without parts and independent. In my view, we should say God's nature is without parts and independent. But I also believe God's loving experience is relationally varied as the living Lord of history.

Dolezal says God's love is only beneficent, which means it only gives. I think God's love should be understood as both giving and receiving, beneficent and vulnerable. God can necessarily exist without parts in essence while engaging experientially in relationship with creation moment by moment. Again in my view Dolezal gets it half right and half wrong.

Dolezal picks a few biblical passages that support absolute divine impassibility. I also affirm them and think they reflect truths about God's impassible nature. Thousands of other biblical passages speak of God's passions, emotions, and responsiveness. Those passages reflect the truth of God's passible experience. In fact, the majority of biblical passages support divine relationality.

Dolezal tries to handle the numerous biblical passages supporting divine relationality/passibility by saying God uses such language to accommodate or condescend to finite creatures. This argument is weak. Dolezal suggests that in Scripture, God can portray accurately divine impassibility but is unable to portray accurately divine passibility. Why trust the Bible on the one but not the other? We all make hermeneutical moves to address passages of the Bible that we think are metaphorical, of course. But Dolezal's moves seem driven by a metaphysical commitment that seriously undermines widespread biblical language.

In sum, James E. Dolezal argues well for why I think we should affirm that God's nature is impassible and immutable. But he fails to affirm God's experience as passible/relational and mutable. If we distinguish between God's steadfast nature and God's relational experience, we'll make far more sense of the biblical writings. We'll be able to affirm analogies between the Creator and creatures, thereby making far more sense of God's passions and emotions. And affirming God's impassible nature and passible experience allows us to endorse a God whose love involves giving to and receiving from creatures.

Concluding Remarks in Defense of Strong Impassibility

JAMES E. DOLEZAL

I am grateful for the good-spirited responses provided by my fellow contributors. In reply I will offer some general remarks and then address a specific point or two from each response. In conclusion, I will briefly consider the relevance of Acts 14:15 for divine impassibility.

Castelo, Peckham, and Oord share the common theological conclusion that the Creator of all things need not be ontologically simple or purely actual. Indeed, each of their positions demands a composite God constituted of really distinct principles of act and passive potency (notwithstanding the current unfashionableness of such medieval terminology).[1] It is the contention of the strong impassibilist that such a God just could not be the ultimate sufficient cause of all created being since he would not even be the sufficient reason for his own being—composed, as he must be, of ontological principles more fundamental than himself. This composite God is necessarily a being back of which we must look for some deeper reason for being. It seems that my fellow contributors, as with most modern Christians, are not much troubled by such matters. This debate over impassibility is as much about asking the right questions as it is about arriving at the right conclusions.

Castelo is concerned to find space that can "make divine impassability viable in the contemporary situation." I confess that I do not share this

---

[1] On act-potency metaphysics see Edward Feser, *Scholastic Metaphysics: A Contemporary Introduction* (Neunkirchen-Seelscheid: Editiones Scholasticae, 2014).

conciliatory spirit toward the current Zeitgeist, especially with respect to assumptions about being and causality. While Castelo is willing to be subversive of contemporary God-talk to some degree, he is not iconoclastic enough when it comes to the modern worship of a God composed of parts. In the end this sinks his doctrine of divine impassibility, rendering it but a rhetorical device to get people thinking about God's transcendence. There is no ontological impassibility left in his position, so far as I can tell.

Oord's response basically argues that if I joined him in affirming a duality in God of unchanging nature and changing experience, then I could have my cake and eat it too. I could maintain divine immutability *and* interpret in a literal fashion all biblical talk about God undergoing change. Of course, such a God would be composed of really distinct principles of substantial and accidental being. Oord's proposal renders God's own nature a cause of his being, a principle or part with which God is not strictly identical. Such a God is not ontologically irreducible and so cannot be the first and uncaused cause of all creatures.

Peckham's response is longer than the other two and cannot be amply addressed in the short space allotted here. I restrict myself to two points. First, and most importantly, Peckham does not seem to have an adequate understanding of what it means for a thing to depend on causes or principles of its being. I suspect this is why he finds no contradiction in affirming God's aseity and primal causality of all creatures, on the one hand, and denying God's pure actuality and simplicity on the other. He simply fails to see that a being composed of really distinct principles of act and passive potency is itself *caused by* and *dependent on* those principles. Such a being is neither *a se* nor the absolute first cause. There are principles of being within it more fundamental than itself on which it depends for its being. Anyhow, this failure to adequately construe causal dependence seems to account for Peckham's inability to see how biblical texts affirming God as the ultimate first cause of all creatures necessarily generate the conclusions that God is purely actual and independent of all causal influence.

Second, Peckham does not appreciate the true diversity of the biblical data relevant to the question of impassibility. His response, like his chapter, brings forth numerous texts that appear *prima facie* to undermine divine impassibility. But strong impassibilists readily affirm Scripture's liberal use of passibilist locutions to speak of God's dealings with his creatures. We also maintain that the biblical doctrine of creation and divine primal causality proscribes such descriptions from being interpreted in a strictly literal sense. In his response and chapter Peckham repeatedly declares the total absence of such biblical counterevidence to his position. Again, though, this is due (partly at least) to his defective understanding of the good and necessary ontological consequences of confessing God as absolute first cause of all creation. It strikes me that the interpretive method used by Peckham and Oord to defend divine passibility would work just as well for one who wished to defend divine materiality. *i. e. anthropomorphic passages*

By way of conclusion I would like to reflect on the words of Barnabas and Paul in Acts 14:15 as they bear on this book's topic. The apostles, having performed miracles in Lystra, were identified by the crowd as the gods Zeus and Hermes and were offered sacrifices of worship. They strongly object, crying out, "Sirs, why do ye these things? We also are men of like passions (*homoiopatheis*) with you, and preach unto you that ye should turn from these vanities unto the living God, which made heaven, and earth, and the sea, and all things that are therein" (KJV).[2] Arguably, one implication of these words is that passible beings, like humans, or even the mythical gods of Mount Olympus, are vain objects of worship. These passible beings are juxtaposed to the true object of worship, identified here as the living God and absolute source of all creaturely being. The contrast between the unworthy objects of worship and the worthy lies here in the distinction between beings that receive actuality from another (those subject to like passions with us) and he who is the universal giver of being to all creatures. Strong impassibility is chiefly concerned with maintaining this all-important distinction so as to ensure we worship the one who is truly God, and not one of the beings caused to be by another.

---

[2]Wilhelm Michaelis says the term *homoiopatheis* denotes "one who finds himself in the same or similar relations," "whose attitude or feeling is the same or similar." The second half of the term, *patheis*, is a derivative of the noun *pathos* and the verb *paschō* which "means basically 'to experience' that which comes from without and which has to be suffered." In *Theological Dictionary of the New Testament*, ed. Gerhard Kittel and G. W. Bromiley (Grand Rapids: Eerdmans, 1964-1976), 5:926, 904.

2

Qualified Impassibility

DANIEL CASTELO

For this volume I have been assigned the perspective of qualified impassibility, given my range of work on the subject. I think the assignation of this view to me is generally appropriate. I am not a strong passibilist in that I believe something can be argued from the impassibilist side of the issue, and the same holds true for me from the other end: I am not a strong impassibilist either because I see merits in some of the claims made by passibilists. Such an orientation puts me in middle or qualified terrain (per this book's layout). I would like to think that my views by being qualified are not soft, which could be the estimation of those who prefer hardline approaches. In my opinion, staying in the middle of the road is not a recipe for getting hit from either side of a serious discussion. My visual of the situation is not one of a two-way street but of a table around which sit a number of participants with varying and often viable concerns. Therefore, I have argued for what I think is most fitting, which would be a *via media* (middle way) approach given the polarization one finds with the subject. In doing so, I may sound like a passibilist to some and like an impassibilist to others—and that is precisely where I would want to be on this topic.

If I am inclined to maintain a qualified, middle way, then why not argue for qualified passibility? Why is qualified impassibility a perspective generally appropriate in my case? In the rest of the chapter I aim to answer that question, but before moving to that, let me offer some broad parameters as to my way of defining qualified impassibility, using as cues some of the prompts offered by this book's organizers to help the reader navigate the terrain.

First, my tendency is to stress that God's emotional life is analogous to human emotional life. Analogies work out of principles of equivocity (difference) and univocity (similarity), so to affirm that divine and human affectivity are analogous allows for a middle way option. Having said this, I do believe that the principle of equivocity or difference is especially in need of highlighting when it comes to divine-human affectivity, partly because of contemporary tendencies (some quite unbridled) to affirm univocity or similarity. In fact, I am inclined to think that the differences between divine and human affectivity are precisely what make the similarities meaningful and generative in the first place. So on this point I am leaning toward the impassibility side of the debate.

Second, I am inclined to say that God's nature is passible but only to the degree that God allows Godself to be. I think it important to stress repeatedly that creation is contingent and that God's actions in the creation are willed and always subject to the divine prerogative. Therefore, in my opinion, any gesture toward a kind of fatalism (that God is necessarily subject to some kind of process or logic) takes away from what could be termed "God's Godness" as I see it alluded to in Scripture repeatedly. Case after case God is referred to as the "Ancient of Days," the "Alpha and Omega," and so on, and with these appellations comes the notion that God is beyond the limits and strictures associated with creaturely existence.[1] Again, this sensibility has me moving in an impassibilist direction.

Third, Christology is all important in (im)passibility discussions, and I find this to be the main dogmatic locus that provides the rationale for pursuing a middle way in these discussions. Because of Jesus, good reasons exist for affirming passibilist and impassibilist convictions. But again the contemporary climate is often one that is exceedingly staurocentric (that is, focused on the cross and other pertinent themes) to the point that other aspects of Christology are woefully neglected. A random inventory of matters that contribute to the ethos of Christianity, such as hymnody and accounts of salvation, can suggest the point.[2] Whereas the suffering and

---

[1] The Scriptural possibilities here are sundry. A rough sampling would include Num 23:19; Job 9:32; Is 44:6; 48:12; Dan 7:9; Rev 1:8; 22:13.

[2] I realize this is a highly unsystematic way to proceed, but if one looks at a hymnal within my tradition (*The United Methodist Hymnal*), one sees within the subject index the following subheadings under "Jesus Christ": "atonement," "blood," "cross," "example," "incarnation," "lordship," "love for,"

cross of Jesus open up space for passibilist considerations, these only make sense within larger framings, including the all-important christological bookends of preexistence/incarnation and resurrection/ascension, both of which (I would argue) have impassibilist connotations.

Finally, God's interactions in and with the world and our interactions with God are oftentimes said to be vitalized by passibilist perspectives, but although some truth is to be preserved here, I believe vitalization is not all that is desirable in such interactions.[3] Given the broken state of things, what is needed is not simply vitality but efficacy. To riff on Bonhoeffer's phrase, I believe that it is not simply the case that only the passible but also that the impassible God "can help" since the help the world needs so desperately is God's—and only God's—to give. In other words, the help God's Spirit renders (cf. Rom 8:26) is a function of God's unique identity and role within the cosmos.[4] Therefore, when speaking of spiritual practices (like prayer), Christian virtues and character, and other aspects of the Christian life, theologians ought to appeal to impassibility in a "qualified" way for the sake of registering some important dynamics, not the least of which is hope for the peaceable kingdom. *application of impassibility*

These points should help the reader see overall what I am after definitionally by allowing myself to be categorized as offering a qualified impassibilist view. The rest of the chapter will flesh out this definition, going into greater detail on these and other points. To get started, we will begin with some autobiographical considerations.

EVERY VIEW HAS A BACKGROUND STORY

I was first drawn to the topic of divine (im)passibility during my doctoral program, in large part because of the work of Jürgen Moltmann. I first studied Moltmann in my seminary days, and I found many of his claims,

---

"love of," "name of," and "presence." Of these subheadings, the least populated one is "incarnation" (ten hymns). Notice that there are no subheadings for "resurrection" or "ascension" (although an occasional hymn might treat one of these topics). I realize good reasons exist for these and other outcomes, but the Christology that ensues as a result of these emphases is often impoverished.

[3] The source of the vitalization here is that God actively identifies and joins with us in our suffering; therefore, these accounts portray God as actively related to our dire situation. The vast majority of contemporary proposals that promote a suffering God have as a central impetus this very logic. Examples would include figures noted later in the chapter.

[4] See Dietrich Bonhoeffer, *Letters and Papers from Prison* (New York: Touchstone, 1997), 361.

especially with regard to trinitarianism and pneumatology, quite fascinating. During this time I was also drawn to the topic of suffering because I was convinced that on this topic (unlike many others sadly) theology was actually taken seriously by believers in their search for making sense of their experience. This came through to me partly out of my work as a hospital chaplain while in seminary. My interests in a theological account of suffering, then, were funded by my praxis as well.

When I moved to my doctoral program, I delved deeper into Moltmann and familiarized myself with his arguments regarding divine impassibility, especially those in *The Crucified God* and *The Trinity and the Kingdom*.[5] My formation at Duke at the time had me reading charitably such thinkers as Augustine and Aquinas, which is in some contrast to how Moltmann read these figures generally. The situation was thus set up for a kind of clash in my thinking and reflection.

By that time, Moltmann had helped establish a working contemporary consensus on the topic of divine impassibility, one that involved several points.[6] Let me simply mention two overarching ones: (1) the ancient church, in its espousal of divine impassibility, had abandoned some of the most important tenets of the Christian message via its capitulation to its wider Greco-Roman environment, and (2) one of the most important of those tenets was the claim that the Christian God is One who suffers with us. It should be noted that Moltmann was not highly original in these claims, but as was the case with Moltmann's prominence with the theme of hope earlier, so it was here: Moltmann's views managed to generate significant momentum, thereby allowing him to experience almost ubiquitous and immediate prominence so that *The Crucified God* (a title having a Lutheran pedigree, which led many to assume mistakenly that Moltmann was

[5]Jürgen Moltmann, *The Crucified God: The Cross of Christ as the Foundation and Criticism of Christian Theology* (Minneapolis: Fortress, 1993), especially chap. 6; and *The Trinity and the Kingdom: The Doctrine of God* (Minneapolis: Fortress, 1993), especially chap. 2.
[6]I decided to write my dissertation on Moltmann and divine impassibility; see Daniel Castelo, "Only the Impassible God Can Help: Moltmann and the Contemporary Status of Divine Impassibility" (PhD diss., Duke University, 2005). I went on to publish a condensation of some of this work in Daniel Castelo, "Moltmann's Dismissal of Divine Impassibility: Warranted?" *Scottish Journal of Theology* 61 (2008): 396-407, as well as in chap. 4 of a more general monograph, Daniel Castelo, *The Apathetic God: Exploring the Contemporary Relevance of Divine Impassibility*, Paternoster Theological Monographs (Eugene, OR: Wipf and Stock, 2009).

a Lutheran) became almost synonymous with the broad topic of God and suffering.

The first point, that the ancient church capitulated to its environment and abandoned important tenets of the Christian message, operates out of a fall narrative that many people associate with Adolf von Harnack.[7] Many theologians prior to and since Moltmann have appealed to this fall narrative because at some level the need for an accounting is obvious: the God-talk (a term that aims to stand for the names, categories, and descriptors used by Christians to speak of their God) of the Bible and that of the ancient church repeatedly sound at odds with each other. On one end one finds such themes as love, mercy, compassion, and so on, but on the other end one hears words such as aseity, immutability, impassibility, and the "omni" attributes (omnipotence, omniscience, and so on). For Christians who have a strong predisposition to claim things about God that are only biblical, the fall narrative helps provide a convenient explanation for the detectable discrepancies across generations of theological reflection. It also creates some motivation for offering a reorienting or reclaiming agenda. One example of the latter is Clark Pinnock's *Most Moved Mover*. Here is a book that aims to provide a biblical corrective to the direct consequences of an assumed fall narrative.[8] The title itself indicates as much as it is a direct shot at the claim that God is an unmoved mover (a phrase with an Aristotelian and Thomistic pedigree).

The other point, the claim that the Christian God is one who suffers with us, is also not highly original. Christians, after all, have debated this point significantly, largely because of their Christology, which no matter how high it arose had to always reckon with the low dynamics of suffering, crucifixion, and death. One point that Moltmann did help bring to prominence on this score is the claim that suffering and love go hand in hand, that the very idea of love requires an openness and vulnerability that creates necessary space for suffering.[9] Therefore, in that "God so loved the world,"

---

[7]For a more extensive look at this fall narrative, see Paul Gavrilyuk, *The Suffering of the Impassible God* (New York: Oxford University Press, 2004).

[8]See Clark Pinnock, *Most Moved Mover* (Grand Rapids: Baker Academic, 2001), 7, for some direct claims in this vein.

[9]Quotes in this direction include: "For this theology, God and suffering are no longer contradictions . . . but God's being is in suffering and the suffering is in God's being itself, because God is

God was already disposed to the world so as to suffer from and by it. For many today, such a claim is not so much heresy but logical and comforting. Rather than a sign of weakness, God's capacity to suffer is repeatedly taken by contemporaries as a necessary tenet of God's being truly and genuinely engaged with the world. Again Moltmann had predecessors here, including some British theologians of the late nineteenth and early twentieth centuries, but Moltmann's constructive syntheses and forays proved compelling to many in the second half of the twentieth century.[10]

I could say many more things about Moltmann's views, but I have highlighted these two points because they are often assumed within passibilist options. From my end, I have not found these points compelling from my doctoral days up to the present. For these (and I am sure other) reasons, I am read as leaning towards the impassibilist side of the discussion. Why have I not found these points compelling?

As to the first point, I am not convinced by the fall narrative that funds much of the momentum for dismissing divine impassibility. I have been asked by those who are organizing this volume not to pursue questions regarding historical origins, but at some level, there is no way to avoid questions of a historical kind if historical readings play a significant role in allowing or disqualifying something to be on the table for discussion. Ascriptions to the fall narrative often allow theologians to dismiss divine impassibility. That, of course, assumes that the fall narrative is compelling. I do not find it compelling; therefore, I find the passibilist perspective as it is often presented with the fall narrative in tow to be problematic.[11]

The second point is exceedingly more interesting to me. Is Moltmann right to assume that one of the most basic and important tenets of the Christian gospel is that God suffers with us? Is he also correct to claim that

---

love" (*Crucified God*, 227) and "Creative love is ultimately suffering love because it is only through suffering that it acts creatively and redemptively for the freedom of the beloved. Freedom can only be made possible by suffering love. The suffering of God with the world, the suffering of God from the world, and the suffering of God for the world are the highest forms of his creative love" (*Trinity and the Kingdom*, 60).

[10]A prominent example of these predecessors is Geoffrey A. Studdert Kennedy: "If the Christian religion means anything, it means that God is Suffering Love, and that all real progress is caused by the working of Suffering Love in the world." *The Hardest Part*, 2nd ed. (London: Hodder and Stoughton, 1918), 41.

[11]For more on this point, see Gavrilyuk, *Suffering of the Impassible God*.

what of the love of the Trinity? includes suffering?

loving and suffering go hand in hand? The answers here rely on how people go about understanding the gospel, how they characterize the Christian God, and how they define key terms such as suffering, affectivity, salvation, and so on. At work in any effort to answer these questions are some broad worldview considerations funded by biblical and theological commitments.

BROAD BIBLICAL AND THEOLOGICAL CONSIDERATIONS

Early on in this chapter I remarked that I do believe divine and human affectivity to be analogous and that I affirm their difference as a way to vitalize claims of their similarity. Let me elaborate on that point a bit more, using Scripture as a starting point since I am committed to saying that the Bible puts forward the viable patterns for Christian God-talk.

The Bible provides believers with the impetus for speaking of the similarity between divine and human affectivity. Repeatedly, Yahweh is depicted in the Bible anthropopathically, that is, with feelings and emotions (*pathē*) associated with human beings (*anthrōpoi*). What is challenging about these cases is that their perceived significance is often directly related to the contexts in which they are read. Certain examples prove generative and illuminating, but others less so, and this is largely due to the real and present circumstances of readers. Picking and choosing sounds a bit too convenient and arbitrary, but one wonders if this does not happen to some degree with talk related to divine affectivity. In today's context, language of God loving and suffering sounds very appealing, but what if the Bible describes Yahweh with feelings and emotions that this context finds problematic (morally suspect, deplorable, or scandalizing)? What then? I am committed to the theological-hermeneutical principle that the Bible is willing to be more daring in God-talk than many committed believers are, and so this scenario—that the Bible may go where some believers won't—is a genuine prospect. Let me highlight two examples that I have repeatedly turned to in my writings to illustrate this point.

The case of Genesis 6:6 is simply fascinating, given its history of translation. As a reminder, this passage is situated between the rise of the Nephilim and the tragic story of Noah. The New Revised Standard Version translates this passage as, "And the LORD [Yahweh] was sorry that he had made humankind on the earth, and it grieved him to his heart." This translation gives due attention to the anthropopathic claims of God "having sorrow" and "being grieved," both registered quite obviously in the Hebrew text. Such claims are not necessarily scandalous in our context, but they certainly have been in other ones. Some of their implications show why this could be the case. Do these remarks mean that God made a mistake and that God is suffering grief for something that God ultimately did? If so, do such claims run against certain sensibilities of what God must be in order to be God? The Septuagint (LXX) translators seemed to have thought so, for their rendering of this passage is quite peculiar. As evidence of the truism that every translation is an interpretation, the Septuagint translates the parts of Genesis 6:6 in question this way: God "reflected/was concerned" and "thought it over." Clearly, we have here examples of mistranslation, which is not uncommon for the Septuagint regarding divine affectivity, for its "translators sought to remove or moderate many of the human qualities and emotions attributed to God in the Hebrew Old Testament."[12] Let us be clear: mistranslation is only part of the story in this case. We must also ask: Why did the Septuagint's translators blatantly take this approach to the issue of divine affectivity? A plausible hypothesis to explain this conundrum is that what is there in the text simply is unpalatable to a particular theological imaginary that assumes that any respectable visual of God could not possibly include that God was sorry and that God suffered grief. What this example shows is that people's precommitments to what God must be in order to be God can influence how they render the biblical testimony. As much as some might like to say that one's precommitments should be drawn exclusively from the Bible, one's thinking and reasoning cannot simply and exclusively be shaped by the Bible, for these are also shaped by one's era, culture, and intellectual formation. The conditioning I am drawing attention to is inescapable and part of what it means to be human across space and time. The point has to be recognized and negotiated rather than denied or ignored. If not, cases like the Septuagint's mistranslation of Genesis 6:6 will continue to proliferate to the detriment of the faithful's ability to hear God's voice in Scripture.

---

[12]Charles T. Fritsch, *The Anti-Anthropomorphisms of the Greek Pentateuch* (Princeton, NJ: Princeton University Press, 1943), 3.

Another example that is significant in discussions related to the biblical portrayal of God's interior affective life (what could be termed theopathy) is the prophetic literature. Let me focus on the book of Hosea since it presents a unique challenge. The range of symbolism, metaphors, and depictions of God's interior life in Hosea is simply shocking. For instance, one finds more similes in the book of Hosea than in any other Old Testament book.[13] Volume is not simply the issue here but also the kind of imagery employed. Walter Brueggemann has remarked that the "plenitude of images [in Hosea] is daring, offensive and evocative" and continues, "Hosea dares to take us inside that complex interior life of YHWH and thus to be exposed to a range of divine impulses not elsewhere available in Israel's ancient text."[14] A sampling would include God's indecisiveness (Hos 6:4; 11:8), anger (Hos 8:5; 13:11; 14:4 [14:5]), hatred (Hos 9:15), love (Hos 11:1; 14:4 [14:5]), compassion (Hos 11:8), and wrath (Hos 13:11). Coupled with all these anthropopathic images is one of the great *anti*-anthropopahtic passages of all Scripture:

> I will not execute my fierce anger;
>> I will not again destroy Ephraim;
> for I am God and no mortal,
>> the Holy One in your midst,
>> and I will not come in wrath. (Hos 11:9)

In short, Hosea has much to contribute to the (im)passibility debates.

One cannot help but have some kind of reaction when reading through the book of Hosea. That is one of its great contributions to the canon, but it is also one of its most difficult aspects. The matter is so difficult in fact that one sees a host of wide-ranging takes on the book. One approach operates out of a "hermeneutic of trust" and tends to highlight the marriage imagery in Hosea in redemptive terms (typically in a manner that overshadows almost everything else in the book). This reading has that Hosea takes on a prostitute for a wife and redeems her so as to illustrate that God joins Godself to us sinners and redeems us in the process.[15] Given the imagery's restorative and redemptive themes, some have been inclined to cast Hosea as "the greatest

---

[13]See the reference in Ernest W. Nicholson, *God and His People* (Oxford: Clarendon, 1986), 187.
[14]Walter Brueggemann, "The Recovering God of Hosea," *Horizons in Biblical Theology* 30 (2008): 6.
[15]See the broad summary of Brad E. Kelle, "Hosea 1–3 in Twentieth Century Scholarship," *Currents in Biblical Research* 7 (2009): 179-216.

love story ever told" in that who could imagine a more uplifting "story" il-
lustrating the power of the gospel than a prostitute/sinner being dignified by
a righteous man/God who is willing to forgive and restore? The unfathom-
ability of the human scenario is taken to be a window into the unfathom-
ability of God's grace, extended to us even "while we were still sinners"
(Rom 5:8). As compelling as this reading appears, the hermeneutical hoops
required to make it work are extensive and, I would argue, self-defeating. I
agree with my colleague Bo H. Lim that interpreters of Hosea should "acknowledge from the outset the impossibility of reconstructing the events of
Hosea's marriage,"[16] for we have very little in the text for reconstructing anything like a story. Furthermore, the marriage imagery only covers the opening
chapters (Hosea 1 and Hosea 3, and there is a case to be made that these two
passages speak of two events),[17] and the female imagery at work is altogether
cast as negative and voiceless. The push with this "hermeneutic of trust"
reading is to make the book of Hosea workable and meaningful for readers
who are looking to apply the message of the book to their lives. That is not
an altogether mistaken agenda, but the assumption of the "redemptive
marriage motif" is precarious and inattentive to the text itself, and it tends to
preemptively overshadow and tame other things in Hosea.

For those who are not similarly inclined, alternative readings of Hosea
have been pursued. Whereas the tendency of the first approach is to connect
the dots into a meaningful whole by highlighting the marriage imagery
found in Hosea 1 and Hosea 3, the tendency of another group is to show just
how scandalous Hosea is through examples found in other parts of the book
(such as Hosea 2 and Hosea 4). One could label their approach a "hermeneutic of suspicion" because they wonder what messages the book promotes
about women, sexuality, violence, and so on. For instance, Hosea 2 seems to
highlight imagery promoting violence against women. Take Hosea 2:3:

> I will strip her naked
>   and expose her as in the day she was born,
> and make her like a wilderness,
>   and turn her into a parched land,
>   and kill her with thirst.

---

[16]Bo H. Lim and Daniel Castelo, *Hosea* (Grand Rapids: Eerdmans, 2015), 46.
[17]Lim and Castelo, *Hosea*, 79-80.

Rather than the "greatest love story ever told," some scholars find the book to depict divinely sanctioned spousal abuse.[18] They would say that Yahweh appears to be a raging, jealous lover who is calling out Israel's "whoring" behavior with denouncements and threats; soft moments like those found in Hosea 2:14 ("Therefore, I will now allure her, / and bring her into the wilderness, / and speak tenderly to her") could only be questionable in light of the preceding harsh remarks.

For those who take the book of Hosea to be the Word of God for the people of God, the admission of such imagery is painful and threatening. Can a God of worship and devotion be capable of expressing such sentiments, which seem troublesome within our context? Of course, people naturally gravitate to regal and majestic imagery—for example, the "Lion of Judah" (or Aslan in the Narnian universe)—but can they handle the underside of their preferred imagery? Hosea expects as much of readers:

> So I will become like a lion to them,
>> like a leopard I will lurk beside the way.
> I will fall upon them like a bear robbed of her cubs,
>> and will tear open the covering of their heart;
> there I will devour them like a lion,
>> as a wild animal would mangle them.
> I will destroy you, O Israel;
>> who can help you? (Hos 13:7-9)

Furthermore, would these same evaluations be shared by those who were the original hearers of Hosea's oracles? As much as we are inclined to lift up our experiences and impressions of the text, we are also separated by thousands of years from them. Femininity, women's sexuality in the role of wider society, what is offensive and appealing—these all vary considerably across millennia and cultures. Again Lim is helpful here: when one looks at ancient Near Eastern treaty curses and Assyrian royal ascriptions, the rhetoric of sexual violence and humiliation is standard fare. His assessment of Hosea 2 includes the following: "While aspects of the depiction of sexual violence in Hosea 2 may correspond to contemporary forms of domestic

---

[18]See Naomi Graetz, "God Is to Israel as Husband Is to Wife: The Metaphoric Battering of Hosea's Wife," in *A Feminist Companion to the Latter Prophets*, ed. Athalya Brenner (Sheffield: Sheffield Academic Press, 1995), 126-45.

violence or pornography, Ancient Israel understood these texts as warnings of the political and military catastrophe that would befall a capital city in the case of a treaty breach."[19] This kind of recognition takes historical contextualizing work, which lamentably many are not willing to render, either at the academic or popular level.[20]

Do we really know, then, what we are welcoming when we say that divine and human affectivity are similar to one another? In our rush to make sense of the Bible's examples of theopathy, do we conveniently pass over or miscommunicate what appear to us to be troublesome features of the text (as the LXX translators of Genesis 6:6 did)? Do we connect the dots of passages a little too conveniently, blatantly ignoring what is in the text itself (as those who operate out of a "hermeneutic of trust" often do with the marriage imagery of Hosea)? Do we react strictly out of our own plausibility and sensitivity structures so as to judge the whole of the biblical testimony impressionistically and on "our own terms," leading to evaluations that simply affirm what *we* feel when we read these texts (as those who operate out of a "hermeneutic of suspicion" often do)?

Cases such as these lead me to believe that the difference, rather than the similarity, between divine and human affectivity has to be our starting point. What we come to believe about God through the collective witness of Scripture and the church has to guide us as we negotiate individual instances of this language as they take root in real human circumstances, both past and present. The way human emotions are valued from one context to another creates a wildly moving target from which some try to build a "theology of divine affectivity." The challenges are vast here. Furthermore, I am concerned about the need to keep at bay the malady of sentimentalism that plagues so many sectors of Christianity. Sentimentalism basically holds

---

[19] See Lim and Castelo, *Hosea*, 64; Lim is relying in part on Delbert R. Hillers, *Treaty-Curses and the Old Testament Prophets* (Rome: Pontifical Biblical Institute, 1964).

[20] As to the latter, I have in mind folks like Richard Dawkins, who throws out the meticulous habits of mind and practice characteristic of well-trained scholars so as to make the following claim that has managed to get some traction popularly: "The God of the Old Testament is arguably the most unpleasant character in all of fiction. . . . A petty, unjust, unforgiving control-freak; a vindictive, blood-thirsty ethnic cleanser; a misogynistic, homophobic, racist, infanticidal, genocidal, filicidal, pestilential, megalomanical, sadomasochistic, capriciously malevolent bully." *The God Delusion* (Boston: Houghton Mifflin, 2006), 31. For our purposes, I find it fascinating how much of this statement operates out of undisciplined evaluations of biblical theopathy.

that our feelings are inscrutable, given, and the basis for how we attribute value to something: if something makes me feel bad, then that something *is* bad (at least to me). The logic holds for how many Christians evaluate God and God's actions. The challenge extends not just to the need for a hermeneutic of charity; it goes all the way down to the fundamentals of intellectual virtue. Sentimentalism is contrary to discernment, to holy reasoning. By affirming the difference between divine and human affectivity—that is, by affirming divine impassibility—as a starting point, I believe some of these difficulties, which are widespread in many contemporary contexts, can be identified and resisted in timely and effective ways.

One way forward on this topic would be to stress the character of God as discerned from God's self-manifestation and acts in history and to allow this vision to function as a kind of rule of faith for making sense of various claims or at least for putting them into a wider mosaic of factors. Such a perspective, I believe, could first of all facilitate an honest and serious engagement with what is there in the biblical testimony itself. This strategy might relieve the pressure to make every piece work fluidly and in lock-step fashion within a tight narrative that dictates how each passage should function so as to avoid scandals and difficulties. And second, such an approach would allow for alternative reading strategies, including literary, allegorical, and figural ones.

With these and other measures, the point can be secured that humans are the ones who are created in God's image, not vice versa. God created humans with the capacity for feelings and emotions, and given the patterns of Scripture, it is not wrong to think and reflect on God in light of these. While some assert that the dissimilarity of God's emotions to our own is about God being unaffected by us, the language of Scripture is much too wide-ranging to accommodate such a reading. And yet, as the originator and exemplar of what is true, good, and beautiful among God's creatures, God's being—including what can be termed God's affective life—cannot be circumscribed or delimited without remainder in light of the human experience. For humans, emotions are psycho-biological expressions reflective of our bodily processes; the same cannot be said of God. We have emotions based on being bodies in the world of contingency; again, the same cannot be said of God. Therefore, human love is like God's love, but there is something to be said for God's love being beyond the imaginative constraints of any one depiction of it. The same would hold for God's mercy, compassion, jealousy, anger, and so on. The touchpoints are no doubt important, but the differences are vital too since God is not a mortal (cf. Num 23:19).

This fundamental commitment to the difference between God and humans contributes to the second point I raised earlier, namely that God's nature is passible but only to the degree that God allows Godself to be. I am sure on this point the reader will be able to detect some variance among some of the contributors of this volume. From my end, I find it important to stress that God is beyond our imaginaries and in some sense our experienced realities. Over the years, I have grown accustomed to thinking of God in terms of glory, *shekinah*, mystery, and so on. Constructs that would depict God as necessarily dependent on the cosmos strike me as not radical enough in preserving the distinction at work in the Creator-creation interface. Creation did not have to be, and that it continues to be is on the basis of the divine gratuity. God in God's very life is fullness and splendor and so *ek-static* in orientation. Divine impassibility is one (and only one) means of highlighting a vision of God's transcendence that works from this account of the Creator-creation dynamic. Because of God's transcendence and creation's contingency, I think that divine impassibility could be defined as the attribute that indicates that God cannot be affected against God's will by an outside force. Of course, revelation history shows time and again that God is moved by the circumstances and conditions of the creation that God brought into existence. Yahweh, after all, made promises to Abraham and his seed, and something is vitally at stake for God to see those promises come to fruition: "God heard their groaning, and God remembered his covenant with Abraham, Isaac, and Jacob. God looked upon the Israelites, and God took notice of them" (Ex 2:24-25). Commitment to God's promises represents a kind of allowance for a give-and-take dynamic. God did not have to enter into those promises, but God did. A God who enters and works through history is volitionally bound by features of that history; in other words, God "suffers" as a result of that commitment. Therefore, for me at least, a covenant logic is intricately tied to (im)passibilist concerns.

THE ECONOMIC TRINITY

I ended the last section with reference to God entering and working through history. Sometimes that angle is pressed in Christian discourse through the language of the economic Trinity—that is, Father, Son, and Holy Spirit working through the *oikonomia* (the gracious and providential order) of the creation. This approach naturally assumes the prominence of Christology, and as I mentioned at the start of this chapter, Christology oftentimes is a center point, an anchoring theme that allows for a middle approach to the divine (im)passibility debates. I should note here that I have often thought of the Father within the economic Trinity as preserving a dynamic of transcendence within the declarative immanence of the triune God's self-disclosure. Furthermore, I have typically thought that the Spirit is One who can help us imitate (in our way) the resolve at work in Christ's life and work as Christ faced temptation, suffering, and death. Yet it is true that Christology is often a feature of the Christian worldview that makes the topic of divine (im)passibility perpetually a challenge to navigate since it is in Christ that we have the Creator-creation interface bridged in a unique way.

This unique bridging can be accounted for (at least to some degree) through the language of paradox. Rather than a strict contradiction, a paradox allows for two seemingly unrelated (or apparently contradictory) things to come together in a way that reveals something distinct and generative. Christ is a paradox, a revealed mystery, in that the gulf between God and humans, so great from the human side, is bridged from God's end. The act of bridging is registered in the form of a human *life*, something that we can relate to given that we are living humans ourselves. The interplay of our faith in Christ with the disciples' particular, embodied experience of Christ creates a perpetual challenge for accounting for all that Christ is. As with any paradox, it is always easier to home in on one aspect or another. Therefore, one repeatedly encounters the language of high or low Christology—language that I myself occasionally use, though typically illustratively and not conclusively. Why? Because notice that at some level, high and low have the potential to break up the paradox of faith; after all, we are speaking of one person, Jesus Christ.

In my studies of the cases in which the language and ideas of divine impassibility are used in Christian discourse, I have found many types of examples. Some sound all too similar to wider philosophical paradigms of a given age. Others maintain the paradox of faith, and these are the cases that I find most compelling for guiding Christians to a proper role for the language.[21] Ignatius of Antioch, for instance, used the language of impassibility in a way that both sustained the paradox of faith and enjoyed a degree of underdetermination conceptually by being expressed during a life lived mostly in the first century (c. 35–107). Ignatius remarked of the physician who "being incorporeal . . . was in the body; being impassible, He was in a passible body; being immortal, He was in a mortal body; being life, He became subject to corruption, that He might free our souls from death and corruption, and heal them, and might restore them to health, when they were diseased with ungodliness and wicked lusts."[22] Notice the statement is paradoxically crafted on so many levels, including (im)passibilist ones. It also highlights soteriological dynamics. Take another example, this one in terms of the incarnation: "Look for Christ, the Son of God; who was before time, yet appeared in time . . . who was impassible as God, but became passible for our sakes as man; and who in every kind of way suffered for our sakes."[23] Notice here that in addition to the paradoxical framing Ignatius again adds a soteriological rationale: "for our sakes." These quotes show that the paradox is not an end in itself; it only makes sense in light of a wider, soteriological framing.

For me the lodestar in christological accounts of divine (im)passibility is Cyril of Alexandria, who interestingly has been read as both an impassibilist and a passibilist over the years.[24] That point alone tells me that perhaps he has been sufficiently complex or nuanced so as not to fit easily within a predetermined conversation. What are some of Cyril's main arguments? Briefly, Cyril is often read in contrast to Nestorius, given that the conflicts between these two (and others) led to significant christological controversies. Both Cyril and Nestorius espoused divine impassibility but in distinct ways. Whereas Nestorius appealed to divine impassibility as a transcendence principle that highlighted the differentiation between

---

[21]For a general survey of some examples, see Castelo, *Apathetic God*, chapter 3.

[22]Ignatius, "To the Ephesians," in *Ante-Nicene Fathers*, 1:vii.

[23]Ignatius, "To Polycarp," in *Ante-Nicene Fathers*, 1:iii.

[24]During his lifetime, Cyril was often read by his opponents as a theopaschite, yet contemporary critics of Cyril often chide him because he was a proponent of impassibilist language.

divinity and humanity, Cyril stressed the unity of Christ's self-presentation, which allowed for such a paradoxical statement that Jesus Christ is the one who "suffered impassibly."[25] It is out of this paradoxical unity that Cyril can go on to talk about the particularities of divinity and humanity in Christ in a way that deepens the paradox further.[26] One pertinent strategy here is to follow the kind of kenotic logic he detects in the Christ Hymn of Philippians 2:5-11: By beginning with the unity of the person of Christ one can then speak of different aspects of the divine and human "forms." A quote that illustrates the point is: "To the same one we attribute both the divine and human characteristics, and we also say that to the same one belongs the birth and suffering on the cross since he appropriated everything that belonged to his own flesh, while ever remaining impassible in the nature of the Godhead."[27] The implication is that in Philippians 2:7, "emptying" is best understood as taking its connotative shape from the gesture of appropriation ("taking"). For Cyril the unity is preserved in the sense that we are talking of the same One who was "in the form of God" who went on to take "the form of a slave." The paradoxical framing then allows for the most pertinent features of Christ's identity to come through. Impassibility here allows for the bookends of Christ's mission—preexistence/incarnation and resurrection/ascension—to have their say amid the themes of his passion and death.

If paradox is so crucial christologically, does it have some role to play in pneumatology in terms of divine impassibility as well? I would say yes, in its unique way. Of course, one sees a tie between the work of Christ and the work of the Spirit in many ways. Christ, after all, is anointed with the Spirit, empowered by the Spirit, led by the Spirit, and so on. We have noted that christologically divine impassibility plays a role in sustaining a paradox for soteriological concerns. Similarly, we could say that divine impassibility plays a role pneumatologically in the way Christ's disciples bear suffering in

---

[25]For a broad treatment of this phrase in Cyril's work, see J. Warren Smith, "Suffering Impassibly: Christ's Passion in Cyril of Alexandria's Soteriology," *Pro Ecclesia* 11 (2002): 463-83.

[26]John McGuckin states the point succinctly: For Cyril, "to say that 'he suffered impassibly' deliberately states both sides of the paradox with equal force and absolute seriousness of intent, refusing to minimize either reality." *Saint Cyril of Alexandria and the Christological Controversy* (Crestwood: St. Vladimir's Seminary Press, 2004), 185.

[27]St. Cyril of Alexandria, *On the Unity of the Christ*, trans. John Anthony McGuckin (Crestwood: St. Vladimir's Seminary Press, 1995), 133.

this life in a way that renders witness to God's faithfulness and goodness. One thinks of those who pray, those who testify, those who sing, and those who comfort as they themselves are broken, hurting, pained, and dying. How is it that in the midst of such harsh conditions God's grace is made available for others? This possibility rests on suffering being a dynamic that is impactful and significant but not final or all determining. Pain and suffering shape us significantly, to be sure, but we are more than simply sufferers, patients, or those biding our time until we die. As heartbreaking and difficult as Jesus' cry of dereliction is on the cross, this prayer is also a cry of hope, that the Father is addressable in our weakest moments and that the Father will respond—maybe not on Good Friday and maybe not on Holy Saturday but definitely on one's personal Easter. That a disciple can lift up a similar prayer and not despair is a paradox grounded in the life made possible by the Spirit. Only in the Spirit can believers be faithful witnesses to the power of God in their broken lives and circumstances. Hope and impassibility go hand in hand in that they point us to things beyond the empirically obvious, to those things "hidden from the foundation of the world" (Mt. 13:35).

THE FUNCTION OF IMPASSIBILITY IN CHRISTIAN DISCOURSE

Much of what I have suggested so far operates out of some basic commitments related to language in general and theological language in particular. For me, the language of (im)passibility is in many ways inadequate to account for the audacious work of reflecting and speculating about God's interior life. Just the dyadic presentation is itself problematic to me: the framing suggests that one must choose between two poles or options. Even with the granting of a qualified, middle space, looming over the discussion and exerting various pressures are the ends of the spectrum. My personal inclination is to call into question the categories and the weight they place on the formulation of a spectrum because the use of dyadic categories in particular—as necessary as they typically appear to be—often occludes as it reveals.[28]

---

[28]For those who do not know me personally, I have developed this theological sensibility in large part because of my experience of being biracial. Obviously, I could say much more on the point, but briefly my experience has made me realize that I often do not fit predetermined categories,

Having made these claims, I generally do not mind being associated with the impassibilist camp in that its minority status within many contemporary conversations allows for a questioning of what passes for conventional thinking. When scholars react almost with knee-jerk reflexes on this topic, some of my thoughts are: Why is there so much investment, and even animus, surrounding this topic? What is at stake here? What precommitments are at work? One way I home in on the assumptions at play is by highlighting some alternative from left field, so to speak. And in this case, divine impassibility is not that far afield in that it is detectable in Christian discourse across time. So why is it so difficult for contemporaries to accommodate it? And what was at stake for its espousers in times past?

I believe divine impassibility can continue to play a role today as one reads Scripture and reflects theologically. For me (and others), divine impassibility has and can continue to serve an apophatic function in Christian discursive practices related to God's affective life (and whatever correspondence it has to human affectivity).[29] Such an admission, of course, means that apophaticism has a role to play in Christian theology. Some do not believe this to be the case. But for me, I cannot imagine Christian theology without it.

I think apophaticism is crucial in that it opens up space in a number of registers. One register is the adequacy of language itself to speak of the holy mysteries of the faith. Growing up bilingual, I have seen and experienced that words have limits. Words are sign constructs aiming to account for signified things. Within this interplay, scales of correspondence exist. Some words fit better than others to describe realities. I am compelled by the point that our words never adequately fit when describing God. Are they reliable and helpful? Yes, to some extent. But words cannot exhaust or circumscribe all that God is. How do I know this, or why do I believe it? Because repeatedly God reveals Godself in terms of presence, and a presence is not the same thing as a word. Again the former is the signified, the latter is the sign that is signifying.

---

thereby pushing me to ask about the adequacy of categories overall. If I—a lowly, perishing, flawed human being—do not fit into categories, is it too much of a stretch to think that maybe Yahweh also does not fit into predetermined categories in this one's own unique way? The point here is not to be projectionist but to identify the limits of categorization.

[29] Again, Gavrilyuk, *Suffering of the Impassible God* is helpful here.

A second register where apophaticism opens up space has to do with the theology-spirituality interface. I am committed to the idea that the divorce between the academy and the church is a mistake, one that is detrimental to both. I understand over time why some felt that the break was necessary (for instance, the preservation of distance that can allow for increased objectivity), but the consequences of this divorce have been dire. Apophaticism has a way of keeping academic inquiry on its knees; it also has a way of keeping spirituality curious and ever evolving. As an academic and minister who operates in both domains as first and foremost a disciple of Jesus, I find these roles for apophaticism indispensable.

But again for the topic at hand, divine impassibility plays an apophatic role by suggesting that the language we use to describe God's interior, affective life is limited. Without this role, we may easily fall into some of the dangers I highlighted above: loosely picking and choosing biblical passages that are relevant for us to consider, connecting dots too quickly so as to project uncritically our own values, and succumbing to the snares of sentimentalism. Furthermore, this role keeps us honest in evaluating the work of Christ and the Spirit. Christ is a kind of paradox—God in the flesh. The work of the Spirit in us is another kind of paradox—God is not only with us but acts in and through us to heal and sustain ourselves and the world. In short, the function of divine impassibility in conversations related to theopathy allows for different turns and for a different kind of thinking and engagement. We need those variances, checks, and prompts, given the significance of the subject matter.

CONCLUDING SOUNDINGS FROM LATIN AMERICA

Let me end this chapter with a couple of soundings from Latin America as a way of integrating some alternative perspectives into the mix of this discussion.

One case took place while I was in Mexico one Christmas as I was working on my doctoral dissertation. I was visiting my home church in Hermosillo, Sonora one Sunday, and a simple and honest man I have known my whole life got up to take the offering. As he began to speak, he started to talk about a theme that on the surface was quite unexpected in this setting: "Brothers and sisters," he said, "I want to encourage you to give an offering out of gratitude for who and what God is. Because you know what? God is immutable. Theologians use this language to speak of how God does not change from season to season, and that is something we can trust in. Just like God has been faithful to us in the past, God will be faithful today and tomorrow. So let us give our offerings to the Lord this morning knowing that he will take care of us as he always has because God does not change." I was simply shocked as I heard him speak. I had never heard a sermon, much less a call for the offering, with reference to divine immutability. Given that impassibility works hand in hand with immutability (I would say the former is a subspecies of the latter), I was encouraged that morning. A term like impassibility can render hope to the hopeless by affirming that God does not suffer in ways that humans suffer, that God does not feel the way humans feel. We humans need a recourse, a source of hope. God is our hope like no other.

Now take another case. Part of the legacy of Moltmann's *The Crucified God* has to do with a tragic incident: on November 16, 1989 within the throes of the Salvadoran civil war, six Jesuit priests and two women were brutally killed on the campus of the Central American University (UCA) in San Salvador. Today these events are noted in the "Memorial Hall of the Martyrs" (*Sala Memorial de Mártires*) just below the scene of the crime, which is a quaint and peaceful rose garden. And within the hall, one notices a blood-drenched copy of *El Dios Crucificado*, the Spanish translation of *The Crucified God*, which survived this massacre in such a form. The volume with its condition in this setting was tremendously impactful for me when I first witnessed it (which, incidentally, was after I wrote my dissertation on Moltmann and divine impassibility). Here we have a work by a German theologian that in many ways demonstrates his own journey of faith as a prisoner of war in World War II, but the volume is here drenched with the blood of martyrs halfway across the globe in a country that was burdened with a long and cruel civil war where the church was attempting to maintain a genuine gospel witness of peace. These priests and women died unjustly at the hands of political maneuverings, as did Christ; they bore a cross of a distinct confession, as did Jesus. Suffering and death are part of the story of Jesus and they are part of the story of martyrs throughout the world, past and present. Surely, the gospel can be spoken of in such situations, but its shape within such circumstances must include solidarity, remembrance, solemnity, and possibly even tears.

I mention these two examples as illustrations of why I consider a middle way so very important. On the one hand, I find that solidarity only goes so far without salvation. We as Christians need to be able to hope in something that goes beyond our expectations and limits. And yet, solidarity is often all that can be imagined in times of great pain and loss, and that gesture is so important to highlight as well—the crucified Christ has gone before us. I am willing to consider the qualified terrain of these discussions, but I do so sensitively out of care for a multitude of voices and circumstances. The image of a simple man claiming the faithfulness and goodness of God through the language of what some call classical theism is an experience I will never forget; but neither will I forget the impact a blood-drenched copy of *The Crucified God* had on me to remind me that issues of suffering, pain, and death are not simply abstract concerns. I champion divine impassibility in a qualified way, knowing that one account or one take of the divine (im)passibility debates cannot do justice to all the ways God is speaking and working in the real-life circumstances that God's people face in our broken and fallen world.

A Strong Impassibility Response

JAMES E. DOLEZAL

Daniel Castelo helpfully raises numerous cautionary considerations in approaching divine impassibility. Nevertheless, I find his proposal of a middle way between divine impassibility and passibility to be problematic on several counts. In this short response I will simply identify a few of the trouble spots in his chapter without attempting a full-scale critique.

ELECTIVE PASSIBILISM

Castelo advances a voluntarist notion of God in which the divine nature (or certain features of it) is something God freely chooses for himself. He states, "God's nature is passible but only to the degree that God allows Godself to be" (54). It should be observed that self-authored passibility is still passibility. And all passibility requires an ontological openness insomuch as the passible subject must be capable of receiving new determinations of actuality and of being moved by some determining agent to newly acquired states of being. Insisting that God ultimately authors and directs the process of his own intrinsic, natural development does not moderate the fact of passibility as such; it merely offers an account of its ultimate authorship and source. Castelo is concerned to deny that God is "necessarily dependent" on the world. What he offers instead is a God who is contingently dependent on the world because he elects to be so. It is not clear how Castelo's voluntarist account can escape the quandary of both divine self-causation as well as causation of God's being through the agency of creatures.

ON THE MEANING OF IMPASSIBILITY

A second difficulty has to do with Castelo's understanding of the term *impassible*. He affirms God is impassible. But what can this mean given his explicit commitment to the passibility of God's nature? He tells us plainly: "I think that divine impassibility could be defined as the attribute that indicates that God cannot be affected against God's will by an outside force" (66). This appears to be a statement about God's control over his own passible experiences, not an affirmation of divine impassibility as such. I take it that any coherent affirmation of divine impassibility must include, at a minimum, the denial that God can experience *passio*. Otherwise the language is rendered meaningless.

Perhaps Castelo has confused divine impassibility with God's unsurpassability. Strong impassibilists also tend to stress the transcendent, unsurpassable authority of God's will and power over all creatures. But we don't characterize this as a productive will that God exercises over his own being. And we don't conflate it with the confession that God is impassible (i.e., not subject to passion or to being acted on). When Castelo affirms divine impassibility, he is not denying God is subject to passions, but only claiming that God chooses and controls the process of his own intrinsic change. Creatures only produce experiences of passion in God because God elects for them to exercise this causal action on himself. This is the volitional unsurpassability of a passible being and ought not to be confused with impassibility.

CHRISTOLOGICAL PROBLEMS

Castelo finds in Christology the main dogmatic locus for pursuing a middle way. "Because of Jesus," he states, "good reasons exist for affirming passibilist and impassibilist convictions" (54). If Castelo means Christology motivates an affirmation of *divine* possibility, and not merely the possibility of the Son's humanity, which seems to be his point, then problems emerge.

First, he never furnishes an argument for *divine* passibility from the viewpoint of Christology. His citations from Ignatius of Antioch and Cyril of Alexandria offer no help toward that end. How does Castelo propose these passages motivate a confession of divine passibility? Each can be read in a manner wholly consonant with the strong impassibilist view. Indeed, Cyril offers a full-throated affirmation of the incarnate Son's impassible divine nature both in the citations supplied by Castelo and elsewhere. Consider the following: "God's Word is, of course, undoubtedly impassible in his own nature and nobody is so mad as to imagine the all-transcending nature capable of suffering."[1]

Second, Castelo's contention that the incarnate Son bridges a gulf between the Creator and creature is potentially problematic. If he means that God the Son, through his redemptive work, bridges the gulf between God as holy and humans as sinners, then I can see no difficulty. But if he means the Son occupies a middle space between impassibility and passibility or that the two natures of the Son exercise a mutually conditioning influence on each other, then his christological model is not sufficiently orthodox. Strong impassibilists, insomuch as they adhere to the Chalcedonian creed, do not regard Jesus as somehow occupying space in between his two natures. Rather, they confess him to be true God and true man in such a way that these are not blended together in him, or even mutually qualifying of each other. Jesus is not ontologically in between the orders of divine and creaturely being, and thus does not seem to provide space for affirming a middle way. In the unity of the person of the Son, humanity does not passibilize the divine nature and divinity does not impassibilize the human nature. Without recourse to a Eutychian-style Christology, it is unclear how Castelo concludes that Jesus motivates an affirmation of *divine* passibility.

NOT A GENUINE VIA MEDIA

Castelo does not offer a genuine middle way on the question of divine impassibility and passibility. It is true that he finds points of agreement with most impassibilists on the question of God's supreme power over creatures, and with passibilists on the claim that God receives new determinations of being from his creatures. But this suggests nothing of a middle way on *the question of impassibility as such.* Castelo's lot is cast undeniably with the passibilists in that he affirms God's subjection to and experience of passion. The fact that he takes issue with some passibilists on the question of God's volitional power and control over the process of his own passionate

---

[1] *Cyril of Alexandria: Select Letters*, ed. and trans. Lionel R. Wickham (Oxford: Clarendon Press, 1983), 123.

becoming indicates nothing more than an intramural debate among passibilists about who ultimately authors God's experiences of passion. For the
reasons stated above, it is a mistake to think the affirmation of supreme
divine control is somehow synonymous with divine impassibility.

A Qualified Passibility Response

JOHN C. PECKHAM

There are many things I appreciate in Daniel Castelo's essay. For one, Castelo is rightly wary of attempts to fit theological discourse neatly within predetermined categories. Further, I agree with Castelo's affirmation that "God's nature is passible but only to the degree that God allows Godself to be," that "creation is contingent," and "that God is beyond the limits and strictures associated with creaturely existence" (54). Further, depictions of "God as necessarily dependent on the cosmos strike me as not radical enough in preserving the distinction at work in the Creator-creation interface" (66). In these respects and others, Castelo's view seems quite compatible with what I describe as qualified passibility.

Yet Castelo also affirms a qualified form of impassibility toward "high-lighting" divine "transcendence" and maintaining the "Creator-creation dynamic" (66). I agree that the biblical concepts of divine transcendence and the Creator-creature distinction should not be compromised. Yet, as I describe in my chapter, the Creator-creature distinction, divine transcendence, omnipotence, omniscience, and the immutability of God's essential nature and character can all be robustly affirmed without introducing the oft-misunderstood language of *im*passibility.

Castelo comes closest to defining what he means by qualified impassibility when he says: "I think that divine impassibility could be defined as the attribute that indicates that God cannot be affected against God's will by an outside force" (66). However, one does not need language of divine impassibility to maintain this view. Indeed, employing "im-" language sounds in ordinary English as if it is meant to negate passibility. Yet that is clearly not what Castelo is up to, given that he affirms such ideas as: "Revelation history shows time and again that God is moved by the circumstances and conditions of the creation that God brought into existence" (66).

Why not simply maintain then, as I do, that God is voluntarily passible in relation to the world such that God is not involuntarily vulnerable? Coupled with divine omnipotence, this view entails that God cannot be overwhelmed or overpowered. God is unconquerable and indomitable and yet voluntarily passible in relation to the world such that God is affected by what creatures freely do.

Further, Castelo pushes back against the "fall narrative," which he maintains, "funds much of the momentum for dismissing divine impassibility" (58). However, the affirmation of divine passibility does not hinge on what view one takes regarding the Hellenization theory. In my view, treating the issue of (im)passibility as a referendum on the patristic view(s) is wrongheaded. For one thing, there is dispute about how to understand the positions of various church fathers; as Castelo points out, Cyril of Alexandria "has been read as both an impassibilist and a passibilist over the years" (68).[1] Moreover, the extent to which the Fathers were dependent on streams of Greek philosophy does not determine whether and to what extent their conceptions of divine (im)passibility are valid.

In my view, the most important question is what view corresponds best to Scripture as a whole. What Castelo has said elsewhere on this point bears repeating here: "With the double testimony of the Hebrew Scriptures and the gospels' depiction of a suffering Christ, there is no question that divine impassibility as it existed in the wider Hellenistic world is untenable for Christians."[2] Further, Castelo adds in his chapter, "At some level the need for an accounting is obvious: the God-talk . . . of the Bible and that of the

---

[1] Paul Gavrilyuk testifies to "the range of meanings that patristic authors give to the term 'impassible,'" including meaning merely "resilient in the face of suffering." *The Suffering of the Impassible God: The Dialectics of Patristic Thought* (New York: Oxford University Press, 2004), 11n29. Further, some Fathers "resorted to paradoxical affirmations," using "boldly theopaschite terms" yet "without abandoning divine impassibility" (89).

[2] Daniel Castelo, *The Apathetic God: Exploring the Contemporary Relevance of Divine Impassibility*, Paternoster Theological Monographs (Eugene, OR: Wipf and Stock, 2009), 124.

ancient church repeatedly sound at odds with each other" (57). In this regard, while Castelo rightly criticizes overstated claims of the fall narrative he also notes that, while "the matter becomes much more systematized in later iterations, one initially can see that the roots of impassibility lie within several strands of Hellenistic philosophy."[3]

Nevertheless, rightly concerned by significant problems with Moltmann's conception of divine passibility, Castelo maintains the terminology of impassibility as a kind of counterbalance against numerous potential connotations of divine passibility.[4] Yet, he also questions the (im)passibility categories, noting that use of "dyadic categories in particular—as necessary as they typically appear to be—often occludes as it reveals" (70). Elsewhere, Castelo goes so far as to state: "It could very well be the case that the language of divine impassibility has run its course and that new terms need to replace it."[5] As such, given that impassibility is not affirmed by Scripture, I question whether the language of divine impassibility conveys sufficient explanatory value to warrant its continued use, particularly given the confusion introduced by various (mis)understandings of it.

In my view, the purported benefit(s) of impassibility language might be achieved by employing other common theological terminology. Indeed, the Creator-creature distinction and divine transcendence can be robustly affirmed without language of impassibility. As such, given the biblical testimony regarding divine affectivity, I believe it is preferable to speak of God as passible in a qualified sense or, if one wishes to avoid the categories of (im)passibility altogether, to speak of divine affectivity as theopathic with the understanding that God has genuinely responsive emotions that are distinctly divine.

---

[3]Castelo, *Apathetic God*, 42. Gavrilyuk adds that although Hellenistic thought was not monolithic, "among educated pagans, whose philosophical views tended toward later Platonism, the divine impassibility [in the sense of being "supremely transcendent" and "above passions"] did acquire the status of a universally shared opinion" (*Suffering of the Impassible God*, 34). Yet, Gavrilyuk maintains, while Christians adopted some Greek language and thought patterns, they did not do so *uncritically* or uniformly. "Impassibility was not baptized without conversion" (*Suffering of the Impassible God*, 15).

[4]As explained in my chapter, I also depart from Moltmann in significant ways.

[5]Castelo, *Apathetic God*, 68.

A Strong Passibility Response

THOMAS JAY OORD

Daniel Castelo lays out a qualified impassibility position that seems essentially the same as John Peckham's. So my comments to Peckham roughly double as my comments to Castelo.

As Castelo maps out how God is passible in some senses and impassible in others, he says he seeks a via media position. I did not find a conceptual structure for this middle way in his essay, however. So I offer Castelo my distinction between God's eternally impassible nature and God's everlastingly passible experience. Rather than a middle way, it provides a two-aspect conceptuality to affirm what Castelo rightly wants to affirm.

Distinguishing between God's nature and God's experience would allow Castelo to affirm the analogies of divine and creaturely emotions he seeks. But it allows him to affirm those aspects of God that are, as he put it, "beyond the limits and strictures associated with creaturely existence" (54). The nature/experience distinction would also allow him to talk about the similarities and dissimilarities of love between the Creator and creatures. In short, my nature/experience distinction provides Castelo a conceptual framework for the via media he seeks.

Castelo emphasizes the voluntary nature of God's passibility. This way of talking about God choosing to be passible (and loving) leads to the same problems we find in Peckham's voluntary passibility. Castelo's God isn't essentially relational, isn't essentially loving, and therefore should not be trusted to love and relate with us. See my comments on Peckham's essay for what this entails.

I close my brief response to Castelo with a note of appreciation. I enjoyed reading about Castelo's background and the testimonial nature of his prose. We all do theology from a particular perspective. And I find it refreshing when theologians admit this and draw from their personal narratives. I tried to do that in my own essay. But Castelo offers a fine example of combining both lived and speculative theology.

Concluding Remarks in Defense of Qualified Impassibility

DANIEL CASTELO

First of all, my gratitude to each of the contributors for engaging my chapter. These kinds of volumes pose benefits and losses to the exchange of ideas. One benefit is that a rigor can be at play here that a panel would not allow—we can quote each other as well as additional sources to make thought-out cases. But one loss is that a genuine give-and-take is hard, if not impossible, to sustain via this medium. This last response, then, involves both dynamics.

Generally, the respondents have not accounted for my sense of how language works and how theological language in particular works. What this means for me is that I associate with theological language, including the language of (im)passibility, a degree of connotative plasticity that others may not. I assume this largely because people who use theological language have used it varyingly over the years in the history of Christian reflection. These are fluid terms, depending on what people want to safeguard and what they want to avoid. Such is the case with divine (im)passibility.

The point is certainly lost on Dolezal. If one takes the approach that "any coherent affirmation of divine impassibility must include, at a minimum, the denial that God can experience *passio*. Otherwise the language is rendered meaningless" (76) then there really is no way to have much of a conversation, either with me or a host of other people from Christian antiquity on to the present. The terms are what Dolezal defines them to be, and within this definitional framework, paradox apparently is not available. Rather than

[handwritten note:] Castelo also makes it hard to have a conversation by problematizing language + not engaging the argument for Dolezal's metaphysics

paradox, Dolezal sees incoherence, and so my view is full of "problems" as a result. Other words must be available in order to account for the dissonance, so he suggests that perhaps I meant unsurpassability at times. No, I did not. The more fundamental issue is that Dolezal's way forward in this discussion is through definitional exactitude and determination, whereas my way forward has to do with problematizing the language in the first place. We are really talking about two different worldviews here and their corresponding implications for theological language. For me, a paradoxical approach is a kind of via media because it keeps both terms on the table in a mutually glossing kind of way; given Dolezal's lack of interest in establishing such a thing, I find it peculiar that he would comment on that part of my agenda.

But why would I entertain paradox here? I do so largely because of my apophatic commitments, which again reflect my views surrounding theological language. Why did none of the respondents acknowledge or engage this part of my view? Whatever the reasons, the neglect itself is operative in some of the other comments registered by Oord and Peckham. Oord offers a conceptual marker to register my concern for a via media, which is an account of "God's eternally impassible nature" and "God's everlastingly passible experience." My difficulty with this two-aspect conceptuality is simply that I tend to want to resist speech related to God's nature and (as Oord latter says) God's essence on apophatic grounds. I cannot rouse myself to speak along these lines for my fear of saying too much. This may sound overly pietistic, but that is where I am. I do affirm that God is relational and loving, but the determinations at work for Oord in saying that God is "essentially" so opens the door, in my opinion, to reifying the terms themselves rather than allowing them to serve some subordinate function within an account of a God we understand in a limited way.

Finally, Peckham and I have much in common, as I suspected we would. I appreciate his language of God being "voluntarily passible in relation to the world such that God is not involuntarily vulnerable" (80). In light of that point of agreement he suspected we would have, he presses as to why I would not abandon the language of impassibility. My response would be: but that would remove the paradoxical purchase of the move I am trying to make that is necessary so as to distinguish divine and human natures. He is correct to say that "im-" in ordinary English sounds like a negation of passibility. That is what I am after in my paradoxical, *apophatic* (that is, related to the way of negation) account of this matter. Without the language of impassibility, passibility (if it is used) proceeds in its utilization unchecked. Furthermore, without the language of impassibility available, we would have a harder time reading and understanding espousers of this language from the past and present. Not that the language being present guarantees understanding (since, after all, Dolezal and I use the language of impassibility differently) but nevertheless its presence allows for a different tone in a conversation, one that I hope would eventually move to the problematization of all theological language. In the end, I am convinced something else will be at work besides terms and conceptualities, and these might be the *shekinah*, tongues, the form, and yes, music.

Is language not also a media given by God to communicate himself, and are these alternate media not also variously interpret-able?

3

Qualified Passibility

JOHN C. PECKHAM

Does God have emotions? More specifically, is God emotionally responsive to humans? Underlying these questions is the issue of whether and to what extent God can be affected by the actions of creatures. In other words, is God passible or impassible and in what way? Answering these questions, and others like them, hinges on how one defines terms such as emotions, passible, and impassible.

On one way of framing the issues, the question of whether God is impassible or passible comes down to whether God can "be acted upon from without" (external impassibility or passibility), feel "pleasure" or "pain caused by the action of another being" (sensational impassibility or passibility), or change his own "emotions from within" (internal impassibility or passibility).[1] Although the adequacy of framing the issues this way has been questioned in light of the Christian tradition, much of the recent discussion has operated with one or more of these definitions in view. Indeed, while strong impassibilists tend to affirm external, sensational, *and* internal impassibility, some advocates of qualified impassibility affirm that God can change his own emotions from within.

---

[1]"Impassibility of God," in *The Oxford Dictionary of the Christian Church (ODCC)*, ed. Frank L. Cross and E. A. Livingstone, 3rd rev. ed. (New York: Oxford University Press, 2005), 828. Cf. Richard Creel's distillation of the "core definition" of impassibility after surveying various views: "That which is impassible is that which cannot be affected by an outside force. Hence, impassibility is imperviousness to causal influence from external factors." *Divine Impassibility: An Essay in Philosophical Theology* (New York: Cambridge University Press, 1986), 11.

In this and other respects, how one conceives of the debate over divine impassibility is closely related to how one defines emotions. Given the limited scope of this chapter, rather than attempting to define emotions in general, I employ a working definition of "passible emotions" as conscious feelings affected by and responsive to external stimulation.[2]

With this definition in mind, in this chapter I will first briefly survey the biblical portrayal of God as experiencing passible emotions. I will then ask how such portrayals should be interpreted theologically, outlining a case for understanding God as passible in a qualified sense. Put simply, qualified passibility maintains that God is voluntarily passible in relation to the world, meaning God freely chose to create this world and freely opened himself up to being affected by this world in a way that does not diminish or collapse the Creator-creature distinction.

THE BIBLICAL PORTRAYAL OF PASSIBLE DIVINE EMOTIONS

In my view, a Christian theologian should have biblical warrant for whatever she claims regarding divine (im)passibility. Given a commitment to Scripture as canon, biblical warrant requires that one's claims are congruent with the entirety of Scripture.[3]

Notably, even a cursory reading of Scripture manifests that God is depicted therein as profoundly emotional in a way responsive to the actions of creatures. Indeed, even many who affirm some form of impassibility, such as D. A. Carson, maintain that viewing God as "emotionless" is "profoundly

---

[2]There is also ambiguity regarding the meanings of *suffering* and *passion*. Some have associated these terms with irrationality, but in my view neither suffering nor passion require anything like irrationality, defect, or deficiency. To suffer may simply refer to receptivity of either positive or negative experiences (voluntarily or involuntarily), the broader sense of "undergoing or enduring the action of another upon oneself." Similarly, passion may have "the more generic sense of 'being acted upon by another.'" Gary Culpepper, "'One Suffering, in Two Natures': An Analogical Inquiry into Divine and Human Suffering," in *Divine Impassibility and the Mystery of Human Suffering*, ed. James Keating and Thomas Joseph White (Grand Rapids: Eerdmans, 2009), 82. Although *suffer* can refer more broadly to receptivity of the actions of others, here I use it in the negative sense of pain or grief. Further, I use passion here (unless otherwise qualified) in the everyday sense of strong responsive emotion.

[3]This involves *employing* Scripture as the unified corpus of writings that God has divinely commissioned as the rule or standard of theology. See John C. Peckham, *Canonical Theology: The Biblical Canon, Sola Scriptura, and Theological Method* (Grand Rapids: Eerdmans, 2016).

unbiblical and should be repudiated."[4] Only a brief survey of the many portrayals of passible divine emotions will be offered here.[5]

First, God is often depicted as pleased or displeased *in response to* human dispositions or actions.[6] For instance, "The sacrifice of the wicked is an abomination to the LORD, / but the prayer of the upright is his delight" (Prov 15:8; cf. Prov 11:20; 12:22). "The LORD takes pleasure in his people" (Ps 149:4) and God may be fully pleased when one walks in a manner "worthy of the Lord" (Col 1:10; cf. Col 3:20).

Conversely, Scripture repeatedly depicts God as deeply displeased, vexed, "grieved ... to his heart" (Gen 6:6), provoked, and angered by human evil. Israel "provoked [*qāṣap*, hiphil, *caused* to be angry] the LORD" to "wrath in the wilderness" (Deut 9:7) and on many other occasions.[7] Psalm 78:40-41 recounts:

How often they rebelled against Him in the wilderness
And grieved [*'āṣab*, hiphil, *caused* to be grieved] Him in the desert!
Again and again they tempted God,
And pained [*tāwāh*, hiphil, *caused* to be pained] the Holy One of Israel.
　　(NASB; cf. Is 63:10; 1 Cor 10:5)

These and other negative divine emotions are never portrayed as arbitrary or unmotivated but are always appropriately responsive to evil. At the same time, according to Psalm 78:38, God willingly "restrained his anger," often postponing and mitigating judgment (cf. Lam 3:32-33; Judg 10:16).

Scripture also portrays God's intense passion for exclusive relationship with his people, often depicting God as the steadfast, unrequited lover of an unfaithful wife (See Hos 1–3; Is 62:4; Jer 2:2; 3:1-12; Ezek 16; 23; Zech 8:2;

---

[4]D. A. Carson, *The Difficult Doctrine of the Love of God* (Wheaton, IL: Crossway, 2000), 48. He adds, God's love "is clearly a vulnerable love that feels the pain and pleads for repentance" (59). Yet he denies that God is "vulnerable from the outside," maintaining that if God "suffers, it is because he chooses to suffer. God is impassible in the sense that he sustains no 'passion,' no emotion, that makes him vulnerable from the outside, over which he has no control, or which he has not foreseen" (60).

[5]For a fuller survey, see John C. Peckham, *The Concept of Divine Love in the Context of the God-World Relationship* (New York: Peter Lang, 2014).

[6]On divine pleasure and displeasure and the evaluative aspect of divine love more broadly, see John C. Peckham, *The Love of God: A Canonical Model* (Downers Grove, IL: IVP Academic, 2015); Peckham, *Concept of Divine Love*.

[7]Scripture often depicts God as "provoked to anger" (Deut 32:16) or some other emotion. See, among many others, Deut 4:25; Judg 2:12; 1 Kings 14:9; 2 Kings 21:6, 15; Is 65:3; Jer 7:18-19; Ezek 8:17; 16:26; 20:28; Hos 12:14.

cf. 2 Cor 11:2), repeatedly provoked to jealously/passion (*qānā'*) by his people's unfaithfulness (Deut 32:21; Ps 78:58). Yet Scripture depicts God's jealousy/passion without any of the adverse connotations of human jealousy, in stark contrast to ancient Near Eastern gods.[8] Scripture "speaks unashamedly of Yahweh's passion, presenting him as an intense and passionate Being, fervently interested in the world of humans."[9]

God is not only the "passionate" God (*'ēl qannā'*, Deut 4:24; cf. Ex 34:14), but also the "compassionate God" (*'ēl raḥûm*, Deut 4:31; cf. Ex 34:6-7). "As a father has compassion for his children, / so the LORD has compassion [*rāḥam*] for those who fear him" (Ps 103:13; cf. Is 66:13). Notably, the verb *rāḥam* denotes compassionate love and deeply visceral feelings akin to those of a mother for her child, apparently based on the noun "womb" (*reḥem*).[10] Divine *rāḥam*, then, is not merely willed affection, but responsive emotion that is stirred and roused. John Goldingay explains that *rāḥam* is a "feelings word" that "denotes strong emotion," the "strong feelings of love and concern" that result in "action."[11]

God's compassion is far greater than even a mother's love for her newborn. God proclaims,

> Can a woman forget her nursing child,
> or show no compassion for the child of her womb?
> Even these may forget,
> yet I will not forget you. (Is 49:15)

In this and other ways, God's love is repeatedly likened to the tender affection of a parent who adopts and cares for a child (Deut 1:31; Hos 11:1-4).

---

[8]The ancient Near Eastern gods tended to be envious of one another but never manifest "zeal in relation to his worshiper." G. Sauer, "קנא," in *Theological Lexicon of the Old Testament (TLOT)*, ed. Ernst Jenni and Claus Westermann (Peabody, MA: Hendrickson, 1997), 3:1146. Whereas the combination of *qānā'* + *b* suggests the negative emotion of envy (e.g., Prov 3:31) and is never used of God, the construction of *qānā'* + *l* suggests an appropriate passion with action on behalf of its object, used of humans (e.g., 1 Kings 19:10) and of God (e.g., Zech 8:2). See Reuter, *Theological Dictionary of the Old Testament (TDOT)*, ed. G. J. Botterweck and H. Ringgren (Grand Rapids: Eerdmans, 1974), 12:49. Moreover, God's love and passion never refer to sexual desires or activity.

[9]Bruce Baloian, "Anger," in *New International Dictionary of Old Testament Theology and Exegesis (NIDOTTE)*, edited by W. A. VanGemeren (Grand Rapids: Eerdmans, 1997), 4:380.

[10]See Stoebe, *TLOT*, 3:1226. Cf. *The Hebrew and Aramaic Lexicon of the Old Testament (HALOT)*, ed. L. Koehler, W. Baumgartner, and J. J. Stamm (Leiden: Brill, 1994–1999), 1217-18; Butterworth, *NIDOTTE*, 3:1093.

[11]John Goldingay, *Daniel*, Word Biblical Commentary (Dallas: Word, 1989), 243-44.

The deeply visceral nature of divine compassion is further portrayed when God proclaims, "My heart [*mē'eh*] yearns [*hāmāh*] for" my people and "I will surely have mercy [*rāḥam*] on" them (Jer 31:20 NASB; cf. Is 63:15). The Hebrew idiom "heart yearns" (*mē'eh* + *hāmāh*) is imagery of turbulent or roaring internal organs, which here "depicts God's stomach being churned up with longing for his" people.[12] John N. Oswalt notes: "It is significant that the attribute of God to which the OT returns again and again is his compassion: his tenderness and his ability to be touched by the pain and grief of his people."[13] The New Testament similarly portrays the "tender mercy of our God" (Lk 1:78) in terms of visceral divine compassion, frequently using the New Testament counterpart of *rāḥam*, *splanchnizomai*, to depict Christ's feelings of compassion, moved by the sight of people in distress (Mt 9:36; 14:14; Mk 1:41; 6:34; Lk 7:13; cf. Mk 10:21; Heb 4:15).[14] This strikingly corresponds to the many Old Testament portrayals of God as deeply moved by his people's suffering (Judg 10:16; cf. Luke 19:41), *voluntarily* responsive to entreaty (Ex 33:12-34:10; Judg 2:18; Is 30:18-19), and even "afflicted" in "all their affliction" (Is 63:9 NASB).

The striking intensity of God's compassion is highlighted in Hosea 11:8-9, wherein God states,

> How can I give you up, O Ephraim?
> How can I surrender you, O Israel?
> How can I make you like Admah?
> How can I treat you like Zeboiim?
> My heart is turned over within Me,
> All My compassions are kindled. (NASB)

---

[12] J. A. Thompson, *Jeremiah*, New International Commentary on the Old Testament (Grand Rapids: Eerdmans, 1980), 575; cf. K. D. Schunck, "המה," in *TDOT*, 4:464. The collocation of *mē'eh* + *hāmāh/hamon*—murmur, roar, sometimes meaning arouse—appears five times, always of intense emotional feeling, whether of God (Is 63:15; Jer 31:20) or humans (Is 16:11; Jer 4:19; Song 5:4).

[13] John N. Oswalt, *Isaiah 40–66*, New International Commentary on the Old Testament (Grand Rapids: Eerdmans, 1998), 299.

[14] *Splanchnizomai* refers to "literally a movement of the entrails at the sight," to "have a visceral feeling of compassion." Ceslas Spicq, "σπλαγχνα, σπλαγχνιζομαι," in *Theological Lexicon of the New Testament*, edited by J. D. Ernest (Peabody, MA: Hendrickson, 1994), 3:274-75. Cf. how the prodigal son's father felt "compassion" [*splanchnizomai*] for him "and ran and put his arms around him and kissed him" (Lk 15:20; cf. Mt 18:27).

This depicts God as experiencing intense, gut-wrenching emotions prompted by human rebellion. The language of "compassions" (*niḥumîm*) being "kindled" (*kāmar*, niphal) only appears twice elsewhere, describing the most intense human emotions, including those of the mother who is "deeply stirred over her son" when Solomon orders that the child be cut in two (1 Kings 3:26 NASB; cf. Gen 43:30).

Although divine compassion is deeply emotional and responsive and God's "compassions never fail" (Lam 3:22 NASB), divine compassion is not *merely* emotional or an automatic, passive response (Jer 15:6; Mal 1:9-10). God's passion and compassion are consistently depicted as emotional *and* volitionally free and evaluative. Repeatedly, God voluntarily meets human apostasy with undeserved forbearance and *freely* bestowed grace and compassion (e.g., Ex 33:19; Hos 14:4; cf. Rom 9:15-16).[15] God's compassion far surpasses his negative emotions in intensity and duration: God's "anger is but for a moment; / his favor is for a lifetime" (Ps 30:5; cf. Is 54:7-10). God's passible emotions, then, are portrayed as neither strictly passive or reflexive responses to stimuli nor unilaterally willed "responses" but as emotional, evaluative, *and* volitional responses to creaturely actions.

In these and many other ways, Scripture repeatedly portrays demonstrably passible divine emotions, that is, conscious feeling(s) affected by and responsive to external stimulation. The repeated depictions of *affected* and *responsive* divine pleasure/displeasure, grief, passion, and compassion portray external, sensational, *and* internal divine passibility. That is, God is depicted as being "acted upon from without" (external passibility), experiencing feelings "caused by the action(s)" of humans (sensational passibility) while, at the same time, changing his own "emotions from within" (internal passibility) *in response to* creaturely actions (e.g., restraining his anger, Ps 78:38).[16]

Conversely, no passages in Scripture assert external, sensational, or internal divine impassibility. Indeed, though an advocate of qualified impassibility, Rob Lister notes, "Scripture never makes a direct assertion of a metaphysical doctrine of divine impassibility" at all; Scripture "does not

---

[15]On the volitional aspect of divine love, see Peckham, *Love of God*, 89-115.
[16]"Impassibility of God," *ODCC*, 828.

supply" this "theological category."[17] Rather, Lister states, "The biblical portrayal of divine emotion is both powerful and pervasive. One cannot read Scripture and come away with the conclusion that God is affectionless."[18]

Yet some impassibilists argue that portrayals of divine passibility should be interpreted in light of other texts that assert divine immutability. Trent Pomplun explains, "Theologians took it for granted that the Most High was impervious to any pathos external to his own nature" because they believed "God was immutable (Mal 3:6) and invariable (James 1:17)."[19]

However, read in context, the texts typically offered to prove divine immutability (e.g., Mal 3:6; Num 23:19; Jas 1:17) actually indicate divine responsiveness, contra the kind of strong immutability that would support the claim that God is "impervious to any pathos external to his own nature."[20] For instance, in Malachi 3:6 God's proclamation, "I the LORD do not change; therefore you, O children of Jacob, have not perished," appears within the context of responsive relationship, evident in the next verse where God states: "Return to me, and I will return to you" (Mal 3:7). The affirmation that God does "not change" here appears to express the constancy of God's character without denying relational responsiveness.

While God is immutable or changeless in significant respects—for example, as utterly righteous his character does not change (Deut 32:4; 1 Jn 1:5), as omnipotent his power cannot grow (Jer 32:17; Rev 19:6), and his promises are unbreakable (Heb 6:18-20)—no biblical text asserts the kind of strong immutability that would render God as *necessarily* impervious to being affected by creaturely actions. Indeed, most impassibilists concede that Scripture does *portray* God as possessing passible emotions. As James E. Dolezal recognizes, "Many passages of the Bible" do "speak of God as

---

[17]Rob Lister, *God Is Impassible and Impassioned: Toward a Theology of Divine Emotion* (Wheaton, IL: Crossway, 2013), 190, 173.

[18]Lister, *God Is Impassible*, 195. Wayne Grudem adds, "The idea that God has no passions or emotions *at all* clearly conflicts with much of the rest of Scripture, and for that reason I have not affirmed God's impassibility" for "the opposite is true," God "certainly does feel emotions." *Systematic Theology* (Grand Rapids: Zondervan, 1994), 166. Similarly, see John S. Feinberg, *No One Like Him: The Doctrine of God* (Wheaton, IL: Crossway, 2001), 277.

[19]Trent Pomplun, "Impassibility in St. Hilary of Poitiers's *De Trinitate*," in Keating and White, *Divine Impassibility and the Mystery*, 187.

[20]This is recognized by many theologians, including some advocates of qualified impassibility. See Bruce A. Ware, "An Evangelical Reexamination of the Doctrine of the Immutability of God," (Pasadena, CA: Fuller Theological Seminary, 1984), 433; cf. Lister, *God Is Impassible*, 204-6.

undergoing affective changes."[21] However, Dolezal and others maintain, such texts should not be taken as portraying God as he is. To this issue we now turn.

HOW SHOULD WE UNDERSTAND THE BIBLICAL PORTRAYALS OF PASSIBLE DIVINE EMOTIONS?

Anthropopathic imagery. Some theologians maintain that we should treat biblical language that ascribes passible emotion to God as anthropopathic, that is, as merely accommodative attributions of human pathos to God. Three of the most prominent rationales for treating biblical language of divine emotion this way are: (1) The accommodative language rationale— the language of Scripture is human language accommodative of human thought patterns.[22] (2) The impassibility rationale—God is impassible; thus biblical language suggesting passibility cannot correspond to God *as he is*.[23] (3) The anatomical imagery rationale—passages that appear to ascribe passible emotion to God often utilize anatomical imagery and, as such, cannot correspond to God as he is.[24]

In my view, none of these rationales provide sufficient reason to dismiss the apparent exegetical meaning of the many texts that portray God as experiencing passible emotions. The accommodative language rationale falters because *all language* about God to which humans have access is accommodative human language. Thus, to say language is accommodative tells us nothing about whether and to what extent it corresponds to God. The impassibility rationale, further, risks imposing a preconception of God on Scripture and, absent biblical evidence supporting divine impassibility, undercuts the standard of biblical warrant. The anatomical imagery

---

[21]James E. Dolezal, "Still Impassible: Confessing God Without Passions," *Journal of the Institute of Reformed Baptist Studies* 1 (2014): 134.

[22]See, e.g., Dolezal, "Still Impassible," 134-40.

[23]Calvin employs these first two in his commentary on Hos 11:8-9, writing: "God, we know, is subject to no passions, and we know that no change takes place in him. What then do these expressions mean, by which he appears to be changeable? Doubtless he accommodates himself to our ignorances whenever he puts on a character foreign to himself." Further, "the same mode of speaking after the manner of men is adopted; for we know that these feelings belong not to God; he cannot be touched with repentance, and his heart cannot undergo changes." John Calvin, *Commentaries on the Twelve Minor Prophets*, trans. John Owen (Grand Rapids: Eerdmans, 1950), 400-401.

[24]For more on these rationales, see Peckham, *Canonical Theology*, 230-40.

rationale also faces significant problems since such imagery is demon-strably idiomatic and thus does not depend on any reference to physical anatomy. The same anatomical idioms used of God (e.g., ears, eyes, nose, mouth, innards, heart) are also used of human agents idiomatically, being widely understood by exegetes as conveying intense emotions without any intended reference to anatomical parts.[25] Dismissing the well-known meaning of such idioms merely because they refer to God amounts to the impassibility rationale.

Even so, some maintain, emotions cannot be properly predicated of God because emotions require corresponding anatomy; for instance, (for humans) experiencing emotions requires a brain. Yet, for humans, "willing" also re-quires a brain and yet few theologians would deny that God "wills" (at least analogically). In this regard, Kevin Vanhoozer notes that although humans can only act via "bodily movement," the "concept" of acting does not require bodily movement.[26] As such, we can rightly predicate "'being an agent' and 'being a speaker' of God analogically."[27] If so, might not passible emotions also be predicated of God analogically?

Theological language as analogical language. If ascribing a "will" to God does not require thinking of God as an elevated creature, ascribing passible emotions to God need not require a collapse of the Creator/creature dis-tinction. What might amount to such a collapse, however, would be treating language of either divine willing or emotions as *univocal* to that of humans, that is, thinking language applies to God and creatures in *exactly* the same way. On the other hand, treating such language as equivocal, that is, as holding an *entirely different* meaning when applied to God, would render such language unintelligible to us, effectively undercutting the communi-cative efficacy of Scripture.

---

[25]These idioms, used of God and humans, include: inclining one's ear (2 Kings 19:16; Prov 5:1), finding favor in one's eyes (Gen 6:8; 32:5), being "slow to anger" (i.e., "long of nose," Ex 34:6; Prov 14:29), "mouth" as idiom of speech (Gen 45:21; Deut 8:3; 2 Sam 14:19), innards as seat of intense emotions (Jer 31:20; Is 16:11; Song 5:4), heart as totality of one's disposition (Gen 6:5-6). On the evident "proclivity" in Semitic languages "to utilize anatomical terms in the creation of new idi-oms," see Jeffery D. Griffin, "An Investigation of Idiomatic Expressions in the Hebrew Bible with a Case Study of Anatomical Idioms," (PhD dissertation, Mid-America Baptist Theological Sem-inary, 1999), 39.

[26]Kevin Vanhoozer, *Remythologizing Theology* (New York: Cambridge University Press, 2010), 58.

[27]Vanhoozer, *Remythologizing Theology*, 58.

Alternatively, theological language is often understood as analogical, that is, holding some degree of similarity and dissimilarity, some likeness and unlikeness, relative to God and creatures.[28] Since analogical language might fall anywhere on the wide spectrum between univocal and equivocal language, it might be thought of as language that holds a great deal of dissimilarity and very little similarity or vice versa.[29] However, I am not confident that humans possess sufficient knowledge of God to confidently make claims regarding the extent to which language *as we understand it* corresponds to God as he is, absent divine revelation. As such, I believe it is best not to adopt any overarching a priori claim in this regard. Rather, toward allowing Scripture itself to function as the sufficient and final norm of theological interpretation, I believe we should take biblical language in its minimal, demonstrable, exegetical sense (in light of the entire canon), while recognizing that our resulting conception of God is unavoidably analogical and thus imperfect (as is all God-talk). For now, we can only "know only in part" (1 Cor 13:12). Yet I believe we have access to no better understanding or language than that which is contained in Scripture.

At times, Scripture explicitly indicates that theological language is analogical—in the minimal sense of similarity *and* dissimilarity. For instance, both compassion and anger (among other emotions) are ascribed to God alongside the proviso that God is "no mortal" (Hos 11:8-9; cf. Is 55:8). The wider data of Scripture thus provides some guidance regarding how to interpret imagery of divine emotions.

Further, Scripture explicitly differentiates divine and human "repenting" (*nāḥam*), saying, God "will not lie nor relent [*nāḥam*, niphal]. For He *is* not a man, that He should relent [*naḥam*, niphal]" (1 Sam 15:29 NKJV; cf. Num 23:19; Mal 3:6).[30] Whereas Scripture maintains that God does not *naḥam* as a human does, Scripture "nowhere indicates that the idea that God does not repent [*nāḥam*] is a universal principle, but always with relation to a specific event or situation."[31] Indeed, Scripture frequently depicts God as

---

[28]Distinguishing between univocal, analogical, and equivocal language has a long history. See Thomas Aquinas's influential treatment (utilizing Aristotle's treatment) in *Summa theologica* I.1.13.

[29]See Peckham, *Love of God*, 171-87.

[30]1 Sam 15:29 refers to the finality of God's rejection of Saul (cf. Jer 4:28).

[31]John T. Willis, "The 'Repentance' of God in the Books of Samuel, Jeremiah, and Jonah," *Horizons in Biblical Theology* 16 (1994): 168.

exhibiting *nāḥam* (niphal, e.g., Gen 6:6; Jer 18:7-10; Jon 3:10; 4:2), including twice in 1 Samuel 15 itself where God is grieved by the outcome of Saul's election (1 Sam 15:11, 35). Here it is crucial to recognize that *nāḥam* in the niphal stem basically means "suffer emotional pain," sometimes "extended to describe the release of emotional tension" via God's "retracting a declared action" such as "punishment" or "blessing."[32] It thus typically depicts divine "sorrow" but does not entail any "suggestion of regret" for his own actions.[33] Thus, whereas humans repent of wrongdoing, "God is never said to have committed any sin of which God needs to repent."[34] Accordingly, divine *nāḥam* differs significantly from human *nāḥam*.

Similarly, divine jealousy/passion (*qānā'*) in Scripture exhibits none of the flawed characteristics of human jealousy, such as envy. God's *qānā'* is his always appropriate passionate love for that which belongs to him. Likewise, whereas humans often exhibit arbitrary or unjust anger/displeasure, divine anger/displeasure is always accurately evaluative (and thus rational) and just. Whereas humans might be controlled by their anger, God restrains his anger (Ps 78:38). Human judges may be corrupted (1 Sam 8:3) but God always judges righteously (Gen 18:25). Whereas humans are often vindictive, God "longs to be gracious" and "waits on high to have compassion" (Is 30:18 NASB) and freely forgives (Ps 86:5; Lk 23:34). Human love may fail, even a mother's compassion for her infant, but God's compassion exceeds all reasonable expectations (Is 49:15); human lovingkindness is transient (Hos 6:4) but God's is everlasting (Ps 100:5). Whereas humans tend to avoid suffering at all costs, God *willingly* took on (and conquered) suffering for us (Is 63:9; Heb 12:2).

Thus Scripture itself explicitly indicates *some* ways in which divine emotions differ from those of humans, significantly qualifying our understanding of divine passibility. No extrabiblical standard of what God is like is needed

---

[32]H. Van Dyke Parunak, "A Semantic Survey of *NḤM*," *Biblica* 56 (1975): 532. Similarly, H. J. Stoebe identifies two categories of the meaning of *nāḥam* in passive forms, "'be comforted' and 'be sorry' in the broadest scope." See "נחם," in *Theological Lexicon of the Old Testament,* ed. Ernst Jenni and Claus Westermann (Peabody, MA: Hendrickson, 1997), 2:734. Cf. Peckham, *Concept of Divine Love,* 266-68.

[33]Parunak, "A Semantic Survey," 513n1. One can be sorrowful over a state of affairs without regretting one's own decisions/actions relative to it.

[34]Terence Fretheim, "The Repentance of God: A Key to Evaluating Old Testament God-Talk," *Horizons in Biblical Theology* 10, no. 1 (1988): 50.

to affirm these qualifications. Further, given that Scripture portrays God as vastly different than creatures, it follows that God's emotions differ from human emotions in many other ways that Scripture does not specify. However, absent biblical warrant, I believe we should refrain from attempting to specify just what those differences are.

In my view, the biblical data overwhelmingly supports the conclusion that God possesses passible emotions, understood analogically. As Nicholas Wolterstorff observes: "The fact that the biblical writers speak of God as rejoicing and suffering over the state of creation is not a superficial eliminable feature of their speech. It expresses themes deeply embedded in the biblical vision."[35] Accordingly, I believe understanding God as passible in a qualified sense is biblically warranted.

A QUALIFIED MODEL OF DIVINE PASSIBILITY

On this view, God is voluntarily passible in relation to the world, meaning he freely chose to create this world and freely opened himself up to being affected by it in a way that does not diminish or collapse the Creator-creature distinction. Because God has voluntarily opened himself up to love relationship with creatures, God may be emotionally affected by, and responsive to, the actions of creatures. As such, God's love for the world includes profoundly passible emotions but is not merely emotional; it is also volitional and evaluative (among other aspects).[36]

Although God is voluntarily passible such that no creature could affect God if God had not enabled them to do so, God feels emotions responsive to creaturely actions that he does not causally determine, many of which (e.g., grief, anger) God does not (ideally) desire. God experiences both positive and negative emotions that are evaluatively responsive to humans. Scripture depicts God as experiencing great delight as well as profound grief but always in a way appropriate to the state of affairs. Thus God has created a world and opened himself up to it in such a way that he can be provoked and grieved by evil, though he need not have done so.

---

[35]Nicholas Wolterstorff, "Suffering Love," in *Augustine's Confessions: Critical Essays*, ed. William E. Mann (Lanham, MD: Rowman & Littlefield, 2006), 136.
[36]See Peckham, *Love of God*, 89–247.

As such, God can be "acted upon from without" and feel joy, delight, and pleasure or displeasure, pain, and grief "caused by the action[s]" of humans (external and sensational passibility) and yet God also affects his own "emotions from within" (internal passibility, e.g., Ps 78:38) as appropriate relative to creaturely actions and his overarching purpose.[37] As such, divine emotions are affected but not determined by external stimulus in a way that does not exclude or override divine volition and evaluation. God's emotions just are God's perfectly appropriate feelings relative to his perfect evaluation of the state of affairs, ratified (but not unilaterally determined) by his will.

Accordingly, God is compassionate and passionate toward humans, delighting in goodness but suffering in response to evil. Yet God remains sovereignly free in relation to the world. Even as God voluntarily opened himself up to being affected by creatures, God remains ontologically free to remove himself from such passible relationship. God voluntarily remains constantly committed to such relationship, in accordance with his character of outgoing love.

This qualified model of voluntary divine passibility avoids concerns that arise from some impassibilist *and* passibilist perspectives. On one hand, a qualified passibility model is able to do justice to careful exegesis of all of the biblical data regarding God's emotions without treating biblical language as univocal. It can affirm, without equivocation, that God does experience passible emotions (including apart from the incarnation), as Scripture repeatedly portrays, while maintaining that such emotions are analogical. On the other hand, qualified passibility maintains the Creator-creature distinction, divine transcendence, omnipotence, omniscience, and the fact that God is not involuntarily vulnerable.

Qualified passibility thus departs significantly from conceptions of God as *essentially* passible or vulnerable *in relation to the world*. God need not have created any world; he could have simply enjoyed eternal love relationship within the Trinity (Jn 17:24). Yet God freely "created all things, and by [his] will they existed and were created" (Rev 4:11). As such, qualified passibility denies any view that claims divine passibility in relation to the world is a product of ontological necessity or posits an essential God-world

---

[37]"Impassibility of God," *ODCC*, 828.

relationship. Accordingly, God's compassion is to be sharply distinguished from any conception that involves essential dependency or posits that God *must* be committed to creatures, emotionally or otherwise.[38]

Further, God's love is passible but not passive. God's love is extremely active and powerful. God is affected by creaturely actions but he is not acted on in a way that requires weakness (apart from the incarnation) or involuntary vulnerability. Even as God grants others power to act in the world and please or displease him, God remains omnipotent; he is touched by the evils of this world but never overcome by them.

In this and other ways, God is not passible in precisely the ways that humans are. Among other differences, I believe God cannot be "manipulated, overwhelmed, or surprised" and experiences emotions in an utterly flawless manner.[39] Whereas humans tend to be overcome and defeated by suffering, God is never overcome or defeated but ultimately defeats suffering through *temporarily* taking on suffering. God voluntarily takes on himself humanity's sin and suffering, being so powerful as to carry all of it without being overcome. As such, God is unconquerable and indomitable but not impassible.

Although some Christian theologians have thought of divine suffering as amounting to weakness, I agree with Alvin Plantinga that "God's capacity for suffering" is "proportional to his greatness."[40] Accordingly, "God does not stand idly by, coolly observing the suffering of his creatures. He enters into and shares our suffering."[41] In this regard, John Stott comments, love makes itself "vulnerable to pain, since it exposes itself to the possibility of rejection and insult."[42] He goes on: "In the real world of pain, how could one worship a God who was immune to it?"[43]

---

[38]In this and other significant regards, my view differs from Jürgen Moltmann's view, wherein "love has to suffer" and "God 'needs' the world and man. If God is love, then he neither will nor can be without the one who is his beloved." *The Trinity and the Kingdom: The Doctrine of God,* trans. Margaret Kohl (San Francisco: Harper & Row, 1981), 33, 58. See further 32-34, 52-60.

[39]Lister, *God Is Impassible,* 36.

[40]Alvin Plantinga, "Self-Profile," in *Alvin Plantinga,* ed. James E. Tomberlin and Peter van Inwagen (Dordrecht: D. Riedel, 1985), 36.

[41]Plantinga, "Self-Profile," 36. Similarly, Charles Taliaferro, while noting "serious problems with an unreflective passibilism," states, "I believe theistic passibilism is defensible insofar as we can understand God's sorrow, not as an imperfection, but an aspect of what it is for God to be supremely good." *Consciousness and the Mind of God* (New York: Cambridge University Press, 1994), 323.

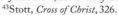[42]John Stott, *The Cross of Christ* (Downers Grove, IL: InterVarsity Press, 2006), 323.

[43]Stott, *Cross of Christ,* 326.

Unlike human emotions, divine emotions are wholly good, appropriate, and without fault. Whereas human compassion and passion are imperfect, God's compassion and passion are perfect, voluntarily extending beyond all reasonable expectations. Even a mother's compassion might fail but God's "compassions never fail" (Lam 3:22 NASB; Is 49:15). Further, whereas humans show unjust partiality, God shows mercy and compassion without injustice (see, e.g., Ex 34:6-7; Rom 3:25-26).

Although God does suffer with creatures, he does not essentially feel all the feelings of others indiscriminately. Whereas humans sometimes delight in that which is evil, God delights only in that which is good and hates evil (Ps 5:4), strongly differentiating him from pagan gods. His compassion on the one hand and anger on the other are always perfectly appropriate to the state of affairs, never involving overreaction. In this and all other ways, God's "passions" are always fully righteous and just, contra the passions of humans and pagan gods.

Understanding divine passibility as qualified thus presents an avenue that steers between the views that God cannot suffer and that God cannot but suffer, advocating instead that God willingly suffers in love, enduring suffering not as an end in itself but "for the sake of the joy that was set before him" (Heb 12:2). God's exceedingly profound delight over the redeemed is yet future:

> On that day . . . he will rejoice over you with gladness,
>> he will renew you in his love;
> he will exult over you with loud singing. (Zeph 3:16-17)

Indeed, even "as the bridegroom rejoices over the bride, / so shall your God rejoice over you" (Is 62:5). The suffering God of the cross does not passively suffer but Christ willingly laid down his own life while retaining the power to take it up again (Jn 10:18) and conquer suffering once and for all.

Only the suffering God who retains the power to finally eradicate evil forevermore can help; only he can finally defeat suffering.[44] In Scripture, love requires justice and vice versa. Bound up with this is the notion that

---

[44]Cf. Dietrich Bonhoeffer's phrase "only the suffering God can help" in *Letters and Papers from Prison,* Dietrich Bonhoeffer Works, vol. 8 (Minneapolis: Fortress, 2009), 479, which I modify here to emphasize that suffering alone is not enough. God suffers but retains the power to finally eradicate suffering.

the God who is love possesses the power to finally do the most loving thing for all concerned; eradicate evil and usher in an eternity of sheer bliss. Love must eventually eliminate evil and will do so.

This does not, as some might contend, privilege God's "will" or "power" over his "love" but rejects any attempt to pit them against one another. In my view, these and all other divine attributes are perfectly congruent with one another within God's nature. God's love, as I have argued extensively elsewhere, is volitional and God's will is loving; genuine love requires justice and vice versa.

In my view, then, neither a conception of unqualified passibility, wherein God is essentially passible in relation to the world, nor a conception of unqualified or strong impassibility, wherein God cannot be affected by creatures, is biblically or theologically adequate. Yet might one qualify impassibility in such a way that avoids the concerns on both sides?

QUALIFYING THE DENIAL OF DIVINE IMPASSIBILITY

Impassibilists often promote the commendable goal of guarding against any conception of God as essentially immanent, passive, involuntarily vulnerable, or worse, some kind of erratic, cosmic basket case. Accordingly, a long tradition has affirmed divine impassibility, in part, as a response to the "anthropomorphic" and immoral passions of pagan gods.[45] More recently, an alternative rationale is the desire to avoid Feuerbachian criticisms of theology as merely human projection.[46]

Whereas I also maintain important distinctions between divine and human emotions and wish to avoid any conception that would amount to anthropomorphic projection or collapse the Creator-creature distinction, I do not think there is sufficient reason to label God as impassible in the context of twenty-first century theological discourse, even in a qualified sense. *Time is determinative?*

---

[45]Thus, "by calling the Christian God impassible the Fathers sought to distance God the creator from the gods of mythology." Paul L. Gavrilyuk, *The Suffering of the Impassible God: The Dialectics of Patristic Thought* (Oxford: Oxford University Press, 2004), 48, cf. 47-63; Thomas Weinandy, *Does God Suffer?* (Notre Dame, IN: University of Notre Dame Press, 2000), 89. Anti-anthropomorphic tendencies are apparent in the LXX, which often downplays the portrayal of divine emotions, as in Jer 31:20 (LXX 38:20). See Charles T. Fritsch, *The Anti-Anthropomorphisms of the Greek Pentateuch* (Princeton: Princeton University Press, 1943), 17-18.

[46]See Vanhoozer, *Remythologizing Theology*, 21-23.

Although there is no uniform conception of qualified impassibility, either among past or present theologians, many have recently advocated that the patristic tradition affirms qualified impassibility and, as such, so should contemporary theologians. Before briefly considering this line of thought, we should note that reactions against strong forms of impassibility are not responses to mere caricatures. Some theologians, past and present, have held to strong forms of impassibility that denied that God can be affected by creaturely causes altogether. Indeed, some contemporary theologians claim that this view is the traditional Christian view. In this regard, Thomas Weinandy cites the Oxford Dictionary of the Christian Church's conclusion that "orthodox theology has traditionally denied God's subjection to" external, sensational, and internal "passibility."[47] Likewise, Dolezal adds that the doctrine of divine impassibility, meaning "that God cannot undergo emotional changes" and thus "cannot suffer" or be affected, "was the orthodox Christian consensus for nearly two millennia."[48]

Weinandy connects this strong kind of impassibility to broader commitments regarding the doctrine of God. Specifically, as pure act, Weinandy maintains, God cannot have anything "analogous to human feelings."[49] God cannot experience "inner emotional changes of state, either of comfort or discomfort, whether freely from within or by being acted upon from without."[50] As such, God is not "capable of freely changing his inner emotional state in response to" creatures.[51] Rather, "God simply loves himself and all things in himself in the one act which he himself is."[52] Similarly,

---

[47]Weinandy, *Does God Suffer?*, 38, quoting from "Impassibility of God," *ODCC*, 828.

[48]Dolezal, "Still Impassible," 125. Further, see the arguments in Ronald S. Baines et al., eds. *Confessing the Impassible God: The Biblical, Classical, & Confessional Doctrine of Divine Impassibility* (Palmdale, CA: Reformed Baptist Academic Press, 2015).

[49]Weinandy, *Does God Suffer?*, 39. Cf. James E. Dolezal's appeal to Thomas Aquinas's denial of passibility as essential to his broader (Aristotelian) concept of God wherein "the first cause must be pure act and utterly incapable of all passive potency" in *God Without Parts: Divine Simplicity and the Metaphysics of God's Absoluteness* (Eugene, OR: Pickwick, 2011), 62. Here, "divine simplicity furnishes the logic of immutability," which "is the unchangeableness of an absolute life and activity" (88).

[50]Thomas G. Weinandy, *Does God Suffer?*, 39. Yet Weinandy maintains, "God is supremely passionate, not in the sense of being acted upon but in a way that is unchangeably constant, as appropriate to a God who is *actus purus*" (127). However, Culpepper notes, it is "not at all clear what the term 'passionate' adds" here to "God as purely actualized love" ("One Suffering, in Two Natures," 83).

[51]Weinandy, *Does God Suffer?*, 39.

[52]Weinandy, *Does God Suffer?*, 127.

following Aquinas, Gilles Emery maintains that passions like compassion "are attributed to God due to the effects they denote" such that God does not feel "sensible affections" like compassion but "acts" in a way that might metaphorically be deemed compassionate.[53]

Further, divine impassibility is often defined "as an aspect of immutability" such that "God cannot be changed, in particular he cannot be changed from without."[54] Paul Helm reasons, "(1) God is timelessly eternal. (2) Whatever is timelessly eternal is unchangeable. (3) Whatever is unchangeable is impassible. (4) Therefore, God is impassible."[55] To reconcile this view with Scripture, Helm employs the accommodation rationale, contending that it "is because God wishes people to respond to him that he *must* represent himself to them as one to whom response is possible" whereas God does not, properly speaking, respond to humans or experience emotions as "affect."[56]

Yet, conversely, if Scripture as a whole maintains that God is emotionally responsive to creaturely causes, should we not question understandings of divine immutability and timeless eternity that entail that God cannot experience passible emotions? Many thinkers, particularly recently, have questioned whether such a concept of God is unduly influenced by some streams of classical Greek ontology.[57]

Conversely, some have recently argued that the patristics actually held a *qualified* form of impassibility, rather than a strong form, and the Christian tradition has been misunderstood and caricatured in this regard.[58]

---

[53]Gilles Emery, "The Immutability of the God of Love and the Problem of Language Concerning the 'Suffering of God,'" in Keating and White, *Divine Impassibility and the Mystery*, 67, 56.

[54]Paul Helm, "B. B. Warfield on Divine Passion," *Westminster Theological Journal* 69 (2007): 101. Similarly, Dolezal maintains "that God cannot experience any change in his intrinsic state of being" and this "is an entailment of divine immutability in its strong sense" ("Still Impassible," 127).

[55]Paul Helm, "The Impossibility of Divine Passibility," in *The Power and Weakness of God: Impassibility and Orthodoxy*, ed. Nigel M. de S. Cameron (Edinburgh: Rutherford, 1990), 119. So also Dolezal, "Still Impassible," 146-50.

[56]Helm, "Impossibility of Divine Passibility," 133-34. He believes "the metaphysical or ontological or strictly literal data must control the anthropomorphic and anthropopathic data and not vice versa" (131). Yet how does one know which language (if any) is "strictly literal" and which is not?

[57]See, for example, John Sanders, "Historical Considerations," in *The Openness of God: A Biblical Challenge to the Traditional Understanding of God*, ed. Clark H. Pinnock et al. (Downers Grove, IL: InterVarsity Press, 1994), 59-91.

[58]See, e.g., Gavrilyuk, *Suffering of the Impassible God*, 21-63. Weinandy, *Does God Suffer?*, 83-113; Lister, *God Is Impassible*, 41-122.

Given the parameters established by the editors of this volume, it is beyond the scope of this chapter to further address issues related to the historical origin and understanding of the concept of divine impassibility in the Christian tradition.

However, it is important to note here that one of the leading proponents of a qualified kind of divine impassibility, Paul Gavrilyuk, advocates what he takes to be the patristic view that "divine impassibility is primarily a metaphysical term, marking God's unlikeness to everything in the created order, not a psychological term denoting (as modern passibilists allege) God's emotional apathy."[59] Accordingly, he contends, "Divine impassibility functioned as an apophatic qualifier of all divine emotions and as the marker of the unmistakably divine identity."[60]

At the same time, Gavrilyuk maintains that there was no single, monolithic patristic view on (im)passibility. Indeed, whereas some advocates of both strong and qualified impassibility claim the tradition supports their view, according to Gavrilyuk, the diversity regarding (im)passibility was such that qualified passibility could also find significant support in the tradition, particularly given the (qualified) theopaschite terminology employed by many church fathers.[61]

In my view, the question should not primarily be which view corresponds to that of the church fathers, who held varying opinions, but which view best corresponds to Scripture as a whole. As such, putting conclusions regarding the patristic view(s) aside, I agree with Daniel Castelo that given "the double testimony of the Hebrew Scriptures and the gospels' depiction of a suffering Christ, there is no question that divine impassibility as it existed in the wider Hellenistic world is untenable for Christians."[62] Indeed, as Gavrilyuk puts it, *both* "unrestricted divine passibility" and "unrestricted divine impassibility" are "fraught with many difficulties."[63]

---

[59]"God's Impassible Suffering in the Flesh: The Promise of Paradoxical Christology," in Keating and White, *Divine Impassibility and the Mystery*, 139.

[60]Gavrilyuk, *Suffering of the Impassible God*, 173.

[61]Gavrilyuk, *Suffering of the Impassible God*, 89. Indeed, Gavrilyuk maintains, even "the orthodox" used "theopaschite expressions" in "reference to Christ's crucifixion as freely as did the Arians" (127).

[62]Daniel Castelo, *The Apathetic God: Exploring the Contemporary Relevance of Divine Impassibility*, Paternoster Theological Monographs (Eugene, OR: Wipf and Stock, 2009), 124.

[63]Gavrilyuk, *Suffering of the Impassible God*, 5.

Moreover, regarding some qualified forms of impassibility, I do not think any perspective that restricts divine passibility to the incarnation of Jesus, as do some qualified forms of divine impassibility, does justice to the consistent depiction of divine emotions throughout Scripture. Beyond this, I question whether and to what extent employing the language of impassibility (even as qualified) provides explanatory value that is not already capably conveyed by other theological concepts that may be confidently derived from Scripture.

Lister, Castelo, and Gavrilyuk all affirm impassibility as an "apopathic qualifier and indicator of divine transcendence."[64] For his part, Lister maintains that God has "actual in-time relations with his creatures" such that God truly is emotionally "affected by his creatures" (analogically) but "in ways that accord rather than conflict with his [self-determining and deterministic] will" such that God is transcendently and voluntarily "responsive, but never passive" and cannot be "manipulated, overwhelmed, or surprised."[65]

Castelo affirms a qualified form of divine impassibility wherein God "cannot be affected against his will by an outside force."[66] At the same time, Castelo is willing to maintain divine passibility, at least in Christ.[67] Similarly, Gavrilyuk affirms that God is "impassible inasmuch as he is able to conquer sin, suffering, and death; and God is also passible (in a carefully qualified sense) inasmuch as in the incarnation God has chosen to enter the human condition in order to transform it."[68]

Yet if, as Gavrilyuk explains, the "modest" function of impassibility was to make explicit "that emotionally coloured characteristics should not be conceived entirely along the lines of their human analogies," one hardly needs the term impassibility to accomplish this goal.[69] The Creator-creature distinction, divine transcendence, omnipotence, and omniscience can all be

---

[64]Castelo, *Apathetic God*, 124. So Gavrilyuk, *Suffering of the Impassible God*, 48; Lister, *God Is Impassible*, 102.

[65]Lister, *God Is Impassible*, 106, 36, 230. Lister notes that, under Creel's definition, this might make him a passibilist (150). Dolezal refers to this as the "voluntarist redefinition of the classical doctrine" by the "neo-impassibilists" and maintains that it contradicts "the classical Christian tradition" ("Still Impassible," 146).

[66]Castelo, *Apathetic God*, 16. He adds "against his will" to Creel's operational definition "because of the conceptual possibilities provided by the incarnation of Christ" (16n43).

[67]Castelo, *Apathetic God*, 3-4.

[68]Gavrilyuk, "God's Impassible Suffering," 146.

[69]Gavrilyuk, *Suffering of the Impassible God*, 62.

robustly affirmed without language of impassibility.[70] Further, given that theologians have spoken of humans as "impassible" (relative to the resurrected state or "virtuous state attained by monastic discipline") I do not see how the term could function as a "marker of the unmistakably divine identity."[71]

It seems to me that emphasizing the constancy of God's unchanging character would suffice to assuage any concerns that God is subject to erratic, irrational, or untrustworthy passions.[72] Affirming voluntary divine passibility would accomplish the goal of maintaining that God is not involuntarily vulnerable and, alongside the affirmation of omnipotence, entails that God cannot be overwhelmed or overpowered, while maintaining that God is (analogically) affected by free creaturely actions in ways he does not ideally will. Here, if impassibility might simply mean "resilient in the face of suffering," as Gavrilyuk suggests, would not omnipotence also entail at least this much?[73] If "impassible" is meant to affirm that God cannot be overcome or defeated would not a term such as unconquerable or indomitable do the work much more clearly?

Given that impassibility is not affirmed in Scripture (semantically or conceptually) and given the confusion and diversity of meanings associated with this term in past and present theology, I wonder whether its utility is far too slight to warrant continued use, particularly if we aim for clarity in theological communication. To his credit, Castelo recognizes: "It could very well be the case that the language of divine impassibility has run its course and that new terms need to replace it."[74] Robert Jenson goes further, stating, "I am more or less aware of the subtle qualifications and real insights involved in the tradition's sophisticated massaging of the notion of impassibility. But in any sense of impassibility perceptible on

---

[70]Divine timelessness (defined as absence of succession) and strong immutability (meaning God cannot change in any way whatsoever) do seem to require a strong form of impassibility. In my view, however, Scripture does not support either divine timelessness or strong immutability. See Peckham, *Love of God*, 263-69, 271. For an excellent discussion of the issues involved, see R. T. Mullins, *The End of the Timeless God* (New York: Oxford University Press, 2016).

[71]Gavrilyuk, *Suffering of the Impassible God*, 15, 173.

[72]Likewise, Taliaferro notes, "Insofar as emotions involve making irrational judgments, these will be excluded from a God with maximal cognitive power" (*Consciousness and the Mind*, 332).

[73]Gavrilyuk, *Suffering of the Impassible God*, 11n.29.

[74]Castelo, *Apathetic God*, 68.

the face of the word, it will not do as an attribute of the God of Scripture and dogma."[75]

If one does not wish to speak of God as passible either, however, why not speak of divine emotions as theopathic instead? As Kevin Vanhoozer suggests, given that humans were created in God's image, "Perhaps the Bible's depiction of divine suffering is less a matter of anthropopathic projection than it is a case of human suffering being theopathic (God-like)."[76] Perhaps, labeling divine emotions as theopathic could convey that God does have responsive emotions while qualifying those emotions as distinctly divine.

OTHER QUESTIONS REGARDING DIVINE PASSIBILITY

The editors have asked each contributor to not only provide a case for our position regarding (im)passibility but to respond to some specific questions in this regard: (1) Is God's emotional life analogous to human emotional life? (2) Are God's nature, will, and knowledge passible, and to what extent? (3) Does human activity (such as prayer) occasion an emotive/volitional response from God? (4) Do the incarnation and passion of Jesus Christ necessitate passibility? I have addressed the first question above. I will now turn to the specific implications of my view with regard to the three remaining questions.

Are God's nature, will, and knowledge passible, and to what extent? In my view, God is not essentially passible *in relation to the world* because God is not essentially related to the world. I believe that God genuinely exercises free will in this and other regards.[77] However, God's nature is such that God can condescend to relate to the world in a way that opens himself up to being deeply affected by creatures. Even as the greater can condescend to the lesser, God can condescend to the level of intimate communion and

---

[75]Robert Jenson, "Ipse Pater Non Est Impassibilis," in Keating and White, *Divine Impassibility and the Mystery*, 120.

[76]Vanhoozer, *Remythologizing Theology*, 77-78. Elsewhere Vanhoozer maintained: "Impassibility means not that God is unfeeling but that God is never *overcome* or *overwhelmed* by passion. Though certain feelings may *befall* God, he will not be subject to them. In this strict sense, then, it is no contradiction to say that God experiences human sorrow yet is nevertheless apathetic (because this experience does not compromise his reason, will or wisdom)." *First Theology: God, Scripture, and Hermeneutics* (Downers Grove, IL: IVP Academic, 2002), 93 (emphasis original). That is, "God feels the force of the human experience without suffering change in his being, will or knowledge."

[77]On divine freedom, see Peckham, *Love of God*.

relationship with creatures without in any way diminishing his divinity or majesty.

Further, I believe the *content of* God's will in relation to this world is passible in that it is affected by and takes into account that which creatures freely will. Because humans sometimes will otherwise than God desires, God's ideal will is sometimes unfulfilled. God, however, *remedially* wills that which is best given the free decisions of creatures, which God does not causally determine. Thus, God takes into account creaturely decisions in a way that affects his remedial will and purpose for history. Accordingly, whereas God's ideal desires are sometimes unfulfilled, God will certainly accomplish his overarching purpose.[78]

This relates closely to divine knowledge. In keeping with my belief that Scripture teaches that God possesses exhaustive definite foreknowledge, I believe God's overarching purpose takes into account all the free decisions of creatures such that, strictly speaking, God's knowledge of all tenseless propositions does not change.[79] However, I believe God knows the present *as* present and knows the free decisions of creatures in a way that those free decisions are neither necessary knowledge nor contingent on God's will. Without claiming to know just *how* God foreknows the free decisions of creatures, then, this view maintains that some of the contents of God's knowledge is contingent on that which is not determined by his will.

Does human activity (such as prayer) occasion an emotive/volitional response from God? In my view, the biblical testimony as a whole overwhelmingly supports that human activity does evoke emotional and volitional divine response. Given that I believe that the entirety of the canon should be not merely *formally* but also *functionally* normative in theological interpretation, I believe this testimony should be taken as accurately (albeit analogically) portraying God's relation to the world.

---

[78]On the distinction between God's ideal and remedial wills, see Peckham, *Love of God*, 257-63. See further chapter 2 in John C. Peckham, *Theodicy of Love: Cosmic Conflict and the Problem of Evil* (Grand Rapids: Baker Academic, 2018).

[79]Contra claims of some open theists, surprise is unnecessary to responsive emotions because foreknowledge is not identical to experience. One may possess *certain* theoretical knowledge of something without experience of it. Moreover, emotions do not require surprise; one might be deeply moved by the second reading of a novel.

As seen earlier, Scripture repeatedly portrays God as provoked and grieved by evil human activity and there is abundant testimony that the course of divine action is affected by and responsive to human activity (e.g., Jer 18:7-10). In this regard, Scripture consistently displays the importance and impact of entreaty and prayer. God frequently responds to supplication, being moved to compassion and relenting from judgment in reaction to human entreaty (Joel 2:13-14; Jon 3:9-10). God is "moved to pity [*nāḥam*] by" his people's "groaning" (Judg 2:18, causative *mem*), "could no longer bear to see Israel suffer" (Judg 10:16), and is "moved by prayer" for the land (2 Sam 21:14 NASB; 24:25).

God is eager to relent [*nāḥam*] if only his people will repent (Jer 18:7-10; cf. Ps 81:13-14). If his people call, in good faith, God will hear and respond (Is 30:18-19; Jer 33:3; cf. Mt 7:7-8). Indeed, in 2 Chronicles 7:14, God states "If my people who are called by my name humble themselves, pray, seek my face, and turn from their wicked ways, then I will hear from heaven, and will forgive their sin and heal their land."

Conversely, divine action is sometimes depicted as being impeded for lack of faith (e.g., Mk 6:5) or prayer (e.g., Mk 9:29) and God sometimes speaks as if intercession is a necessary condition of his favorable action. One striking instance of this is found in Ezekiel 22:30, wherein God states, "And I sought for anyone among them who would repair the wall and stand in the breach before me on behalf of the land, so that I would not destroy it; but I found no one" (cf. Is 63:5). Notably Christ, the ultimate intercessor who "always lives to make intercession" for us (Heb 7:25), taught humans to pray that God's will be done (Mt 6:10), modeled a life of intercessory prayer (e.g., Lk 22:32; 23:34) and taught his disciples to do likewise, and emphasized that believers should "ask, and it will be given you" (Mt 7:7; cf. Lk 11:5-13; Jn 16:23).

Many more examples of divine emotive/volitional response to human action could be cited here. For now, suffice it to say that because God has created a world wherein creatures possess freedom and God has opened himself up to being affected by creaturely causes, all human activity has implications for God's will and God's emotions. As noted earlier, I believe God's overarching (remedial) will takes into account all the free decisions of creatures and that God is deeply affected (analogically) by human actions. What humans believe, will, and do really matters to God.

Do the incarnation and passion of Jesus Christ necessitate passibility? If passibility is minimally defined as being affected by creaturely causes, it seems to me that the incarnation and passion of Christ do necessitate at least the conclusion that God *can* open himself up to a state of passible relationship with the world and *has done so*. In my view, Christ's incarnation and passion demonstrate that the second person of the Trinity voluntarily condescended to take on humanity and make himself susceptible to things he was otherwise not susceptible to (hunger, thirst, fatigue, etc.), while remaining fully divine and without in any way diminishing his divinity (Phil 2:6-8). Given a single-subject Christology, this voluntary condescension of Christ evinces that the divine nature is compatible with passibility; the kinds of things Christ experienced evinces that God in Christ experienced passible emotions, that is, emotions responsive to stimuli.

Gavrilyuk's work is quite helpful here as it emphasizes why it is so problematic to maintain that Christ did not really suffer (Docetism), that Christ was not fully divine (Arianism), or that Christ's "divine actions and human experiences have different subjects" (Nestorianism).[80] Here maintaining that Christ only suffered in his humanity would imply that the cross involved merely a human sacrifice and a human Savior, jeopardizing "the paradox of the incarnation" by "undercut[ting] the intimacy of God's involvement."[81] In this, and many other respects, I find any move to restrict the suffering of Christ to his humanity to be deeply problematic, Christologically and soteriologically.

Whatever one says about the suffering of Christ, one should not make any moves that would jeopardize a single-subject Christology, which (on Gavrilyuk's reading of Cyril of Alexandria) requires some form of "qualified passibility."[82] Further, one should make no moves toward downplaying the

---

[80]Gavrilyuk, *Suffering of the Impassible God*, 173.

[81]Gavrilyuk, *Suffering of the Impassible God*, 99.

[82]Gavrilyuk, *Suffering of the Impassible God*, 150. Gavrilyuk contends that Cyril affirmed "both qualified divine impassibility and qualified divine passibility" to protect both that the "incarnate was truly God" and that "God truly submitted himself to the conditions of the incarnation." Although I agree with much of Cyril's way of navigating the difficulties with respect to Christ's suffering, I think the use of impassibility language is not necessary *today* to uphold the full divinity of Christ and other divine distinctives. Rather than saying "the Impassible suffered," I would

suffering of the Son of God. As Fleming Rutledge well notes: "In the Apostles' and Nicene Creeds, the only word used in connection with the entire span of Jesus' life is 'suffered.'"[83]

Some maintain, however, that divinity experienced passible emotions *only* in and through the incarnation of Jesus. However, as briefly seen earlier, there is strong biblical evidence that God, prior to the birth of Jesus, experienced profoundly passible emotions responsive to human activity. Moreover, many such emotions attributed to God in the Old Testament correspond very closely with those exhibited by Christ in the New Testament. In this regard, if the second person of the Trinity could lower himself to take on humanity without being any less divine, why could God not open himself to passible relationship with the world apart from the incarnation?

One worry is that if God was already (or naturally) passible in the way Jesus of Nazareth was passible, then Christ's "assumption of humanity" would be "superfluous."[84] However, maintaining that God is passible in relation to the world apart from the incarnation of Jesus need not entail that God is passible apart from the incarnation in just the same way as Jesus of Nazareth.

In my view, God condescended and voluntarily opened himself up to passible relationship with the world from the beginning of creation, but the incarnation of Christ was an additional voluntary condescension of the second person unlike any other.[85] As such, Christ made himself passible and vulnerable in ways that God otherwise is not, such as susceptibility to (among other things) hunger, thirst, fatigue, flogging, and even crucifixion. My conception of voluntary divine passibility, then, neither limits divine passibility to the incarnation nor maintains that God is passible apart from the incarnation in the same manner as Christ in the incarnation.

---

say (in the present context) that Christ voluntary condescended to suffer in ways that he could not have suffered without taking on humanity.

[83]Fleming Rutledge, *The Crucifixion: Understanding the Death of Christ* (Grand Rapids: Eerdmans, 2015), 56.

[84]Gavrilyuk, *Suffering of the Impassible God*, 159.

[85]Contra patripassianism, the Father did not suffer on the cross or take on human experience. On the importance of distinguishing "God's suffering as human from his suffering as God," see Richard Bauckham, "In Defence of *The Crucified God*," in Cameron, *The Power and Weakness of God*, 112-13.

It is notable here that Christ's passibility and suffering are explicitly identified in Scripture as voluntary and in direct accordance with God's plan (see, e.g., Acts 4:27-28). Jesus proclaims, "I lay down my life in order to take it up again. No one takes it from me, but I lay it down of my own accord. I have power to lay it down, and I have power to take it up again" (Jn 10:17-18). Further, Jesus told Pilate, "You would have no power over me unless it had been given you from above" (Jn 19:11). Christ was no involuntary victim. No creaturely power prevented Christ from coming down off the cross. Christ suffered and laid down his life willingly: "For the sake of the joy that was set before him [he] endured the cross" (Heb 12:2), evincing the *voluntary* passibility of the Son of God.

Christ's condescension was not only voluntary but also temporary. Although the suffering of Christ by itself would do little good for those mired in suffering, the crucified Lord did not remain in the tomb but rose from the dead and the resurrected Lord will finally conquer suffering, death, and all evil forevermore (Rev 21:4).

CONCLUSION

This chapter surveyed the biblical portrayals of passible divine emotions and suggested they should be understood as accurately conveying divine emotions as externally, sensationally, and internally passible, yet analogical to those of humans, with attention to the way that Scripture itself qualifies divine emotions. This reading supports a model of qualified divine passibility wherein God is voluntarily passible in relation to the world, meaning (among other things) that God freely chose to create and open himself up to being affected by this world in a way that does not diminish or collapse the Creator-creature distinction.[86]

---

[86]Thanks to R. T. Mullins for his helpful comments on an earlier version of this chapter.

A Strong Impassibility Response

JAMES E. DOLEZAL

John C. Peckham's argument for divine passibility is that it makes the best sense of the biblical data. His demand for biblical warrant deserves to be taken seriously by all Christian theologians. The difficulty arises, however, in the identification and interpretation of relevant data. What is omitted from consideration can often be as crucial as what is included. It is in this connection that I register a few objections to Peckham's passibilist conclusion.

CREATOR-CREATURE DISTINCTION

Peckham's interpretation of the biblical text is adversely prejudiced by the fact that he does not employ the Creator-creature distinction as a hermeneutical *principle*. The Creator-creature distinction ought to stand on both ends of the hermeneutical process, as both a principle and conclusion. The knowledge of this distinction—derived by humans from God's true, clear, and authoritative self-disclosure in the things that are made (Rom 1:19-20)—precedes Scripture and is brought to the text as a lens by which we are able to make assessments about the literal or figurative quality of the Bible's varied statements about God. A fundamental feature of this naturally known distinction is that God is not situated ontologically among those things that are caused to be. A necessary implication of this basic truth is that God is unmoved in his being and is utterly self-sufficient in all that he is.

If one approaches the biblical text without presupposing this all-important distinction, the likelihood of misinterpretation is exponentially amplified. This is because the Bible, as a redemptive-historical record detailing the providential unfolding of God's salvific purpose, generally speaks from the ordinary viewpoint of humans as they experience the effects of God's judgment or salvation sequentially in time and space. God is pleased to clothe his own covenantal self-revelation in the customary language of human passions, bodily parts and functions, experiences of time, manners of warfare, and so forth. Unless one were already committed to the axiom that God is not in any way caused to be, such passages might easily be read as suggesting that God is changeable, material, temporal, and the like— perhaps like approaching Solomon's temple and the thick glory-cloud of God's manifested presence within it and concluding that God was therein contained and accommodated by human provisions (see 1 Kings 8:10-12, 27; Acts 17:24-25).

Peckham is right to demand biblical warrant for claims about impassibility/passibility. Yet omission of the Creator-creature distinction as a hermeneutical principle (even if affirming it as a hermeneutical conclusion) renders such warrant difficult to furnish. Specifically, it muddles the process by which we judge certain texts to be speaking metaphorically or literally by suspending a key interpretive criterion. Also, by excluding the witness of natural theology and its claims respecting the existence and essence of God, Peckham deprives the (professed) biblical warrant for impassibility of an important corroborative voice. Scripture is the supreme judge in all doctrinal controversies about God's nature. But it is not the only judge, as Peckham's approach seems to presume.

EXCLUSION OF RELEVANT BIBLICAL DATA

Peckham also overlooks a host of biblical teachings that help ground divine impassibility and which arguably undermine the notion of a passible God. He confines his focus almost entirely to a handful of passages in which God is said not to change. I find these claims, taken in isolation, to be underdeterminative for either side in this controversy, even if prima facie they appear to support the impassibilist viewpoint.

Among the elements of biblical data Peckham fails to consider are straightforward denials that God receives the actions of humans on himself, such as that found in Elihu's wisdom discourse in Job 35:5-8. Also omitted

Decent point on a necessary entailment of a text

are passages that speak of God's fullness of being, such as Isaiah 44:6 ("I am the first and I am the last") and Revelation 22:13 ("I am the Alpha and the Omega, the first and the last, the beginning and the end"). How could God actually be the beginning and the end if he receives new determinations of being from his creatures, which he must if he experiences passion? Every action that befell him would move him toward some ontological end of being with which he was not eternally identical.

Perhaps the most significant biblical warrant for divine impassibility derives from the doctrine of creation, together with its good and necessary consequences. This too is passed over by Peckham. Scripture depicts God as the first and absolute sufficient cause of all creaturely being (see, e.g., Neh 9:6; Acts 17:25, 28; Rom 4:17; 11:36; Col 1:16; Rev 4:11). In order to be such, God must also be the sufficient reason for his own being, irreducible to principles more fundamental than himself. But a passible God is reducible in precisely this way inasmuch as he must be composed of really distinct principles of act and passive potency. All composite beings depend on their parts as so many causes. Passibility, thus, necessarily renders God causally dependent on that which is not God.

Though Peckham offers no elaboration of his position in precise ontological terms, I propose that the reason he is unbothered by the notion of creatures causing God to be in some way—God "has opened himself up to being affected by creaturely causes" (110)—is because he already implicitly accepts a view of God as one of the beings that are caused to be, namely, as a being composed of principles (act and passive potency) more fundamental than himself. Peckham's voluntarist explanation that the creature's actualization of God comes about as a result of God's will does nothing to change the fact that his position must affirm the creature as a cause of God's being in some respect. For Peckham, God is *our* ontological effect and handiwork to the extent he chooses to be.

Peckham repeatedly affirms the Creator-creature distinction. But it seems entirely fair to ask whether he has rightly understood it given that he locates God among the beings that are caused to be by another. He does this implicitly in his acceptance of act-potency composition in God, and explicitly in his affirmation that creatures are causes of God's actuality in some measure.

A Qualified Impassibility Response

DANIEL CASTELO

I had some ideas about how the first chapters I have mentioned would go, but I was particularly curious to see how Peckham would develop his views since his position is meant to touch closest to mine in terms of moving toward the middle.

In many ways, Peckham's piece functions as an appropriate middle chapter within the spectrum in that he attempts to account for both extremes of the debate and tries to expose the strengths and weaknesses of each. He makes a helpful orienting claim early in his chapter when he says, "Put simply, qualified passibility maintains that God is voluntarily passible in relation to the world, meaning God freely chose to create this world and freely opened himself up to being affected by this world in a way that does not diminish or collapse the Creator-creature distinction" (88). Time and time again, Peckham shows himself to be judicious and willing to account for some of the nuances of the debate.

Peckham does much in surveying the biblical witness, which is helpful in many ways, and he also attends to the analogical nature of theological speech, which I again find to be a strength. Of course, when one opens the door in this manner, the pressing concern may be that if such speech is analogical, then what secures it? In response, Peckham's tendency is to affirm the character and shape of the biblical witness: Scripture indicates at times that God's emotions are similar and different from human emotions. "However, absent biblical warrant," he remarks, "I believe we should refrain from attempting to specify just what those differences are" (98). A statement like this appears to me to operate out of a particular understanding of Scripture, one that I find to be difficult to sustain, at least for myself. To say that Scripture provides warrant for a position, such as (im)passibility, without the accompanying work of contextualizing those claims within their own native contexts (which certainly vary across the testaments) is to operate out of an approach to Scripture that neglects its contextual complexity, its cultural embeddedness, its scandalizing particularity. The examples I raised in my chapter point to this challenge. In offering a biblical account of divine (im)passibility, we come with our culturally-based biases, and the text's contexts come with theirs. Biblical warrants for theopathic language, then, cannot be pursued apart from these kinds of contextual considerations. In an important sense, then, the Bible cannot establish a kind of (im)passibilist baseline when the biblical writers reflected assumptions that we may not share with them today. The example of Hosea, one of many, illustrates the point.

Finally, Peckham does not believe that divine impassibility, even in a qualified sense, is sufficiently warranted for use today. One pivotal argument in support of this claim is when he cites Paul Gavrilyuk on the following point, "Yet if . . . the 'modest' function of impassibility was to make explicit 'that emotionally coloured characteristics should not be conceived entirely along the lines of their human analogies,' one hardly needs the term impassibility to accomplish this goal" (106). Peckham continues, "The Creator-creation distinction, divine transcendence, omnipotence, omniscience can all be robustly affirmed without language of *im*passibility" (106-7, emphasis added). My overall response to this evaluation is that Gavrilyuk's point is that *language of affectivity* in God-talk (and this language in particular) has to be disciplined, and impassibility can do that work. It seems that Peckham is inclined to believe that speaking of the analogical character of theological language does that work adequately. I would say, maybe, maybe not. Recognition of the analogical constitution of theological speech is an appropriate step, of course, but the recognition does not guarantee that the analogical point will make a difference in each and every relevant case. For the sake of extending this analogical point, I am always willing to flip terms in God-talk on their head (especially if their flipped versions also have been used in Christian antiquity). The term is ready to be flipped as it stands with the addition of those two prefixed letters (*im*), and these just might do the trick to aid one in the process of recognizing within the realm of divine affectivity just how bizarre, strange, wonderful, and glorious the God of Christian worship truly is. These letters certainly did that for me.

Castelo is using the term differently
than Dolezal, maybe even pechham.

A Strong Passibility Response

THOMAS JAY OORD

My view of God's passibility shares much in common with John C. Peckham's view. I agree, for instance, when he defends a passible and emotion-laden God biblically. Peckham rightly says that divine passibility does not mean God can become essentially compromised: God is, as he puts it, "unconquerable and indomitable but not impassible" (100). He rightly says that unlike human emotions, God's emotions are wholly good. Peckham values Creator-creature analogies, as do I. I was happy that Peckham argues for the constancy of God's character (what I call God's "nature") as a way to account for biblical statements about God's impassibility. I could go on and on about the commonalities between Peckham's view and mine. But let me move to our differences. In a book comparing views, that's more interesting!

One begins to see our differences when Peckham describes his qualified model of divine passibility. "God is voluntarily passible in relation to the world," he argues, "meaning [God] freely chose to create this world and freely opened himself up to being affected by it in a way that does not diminish or collapse the Creator-creature distinction" (98). Peckham stresses that God "remains sovereignly free in relation to the world," which means God is "ontologically free to remove himself from such passible relationship" (99).

Peckham goes on to differentiate his view from my own. "Qualified passibility thus departs significantly from conceptions of God as *essentially* passible or vulnerable *in relation to the world*," says Peckham. "God need not have created any world; he could have simply enjoyed eternal love relationship within the Trinity" (99). This fits what I call in my chapter a strong view of divine passibility when it comes to trinitarian relations. But Peckham thinks God's relationship with creation is voluntary and weak rather than essential and necessary.

The "qualified" element in Peckham's view entails some disturbing conclusions. His view suggests that nothing—not even God's own nature—compels God necessarily to receive from creatures. Nothing requires God to listen, respond, empathize, or be affected by us. God need not receive anything from creaturely others. In short, God does *not* essentially love the world, if love involves giving and receiving.

Peckham's model says God could freely decide today to give up on the creation project. "To hell with you all," God could say. God could freely stop listening in love, stop being vulnerable, stop receiving our prayers, and stop being compassionate. Who knows, perhaps God has done this in the past. God is not essentially committed to loving creation, because God's nature doesn't include creaturely love. but that's why he covenates!

If love involves giving and receiving, the best we can say about the God that Peckham describes is this: "God may or may not love us." It just depends. On what does it depend? God's arbitrary decision. God arbitrarily decides whether to love us.

It may sound harsh to say Peckham's view entails that God's love for us is "arbitrary." But "arbitrary" seems the most appropriate. Remember, Peckham denies that God necessarily relates to the world. His view emphasizes the radical freedom of God vis-á-vis the world. God's receiving love is only temporary with regard to us. God voluntarily—not out of God's nature of necessary love for others—relates and love us.

Peckham could have appealed to other factors that necessitate God's love for creation. He could appeal to metaphysical laws to which God must comply, for instance. He could also appeal to forces and powers external to God that would require God to love. But I don't think he'd be wise to make these appeals, and I doubt he's attracted to them. I'm not.

So, in Peckham's view, what compels God to love us? Nothing. Not even God's nature. After all, "love for creation" is not a necessary aspect of God's nature. God may or may not decide to engage in giving and receiving love with creation. It depends on nothing but an arbitrary decision.

In my own essay, I propose how to solve this problem, and my position does *not* imply that God arbitrarily loves us. I say giving and receiving love is an aspect of God's eternal nature, and this love comes logically first in God. God's love for creatures logically precedes God's sovereign will. Consequently, God is essentially passible in relation to creation. God *must* love us, because loving creation is part of what it means to be God. That's just who God is.

I've presented this "love logically precedes power in God's nature" view in other books. Peckham has read my work, and he seems to address my idea when he writes the following:

> [The qualified passibility view] does not, as some might contend, privilege God's 'will' or 'power' over his 'love' but rejects any attempt to pit them against one another. In my view, these and all other divine attributes are perfectly congruent with one another within God's nature. God's love, as I have argued extensively elsewhere, is volitional and God's will is loving (102).

Before responding to the problem with Peckham's statement, let me say that I also don't pit divine attributes against one another. I think God's attributes are perfectly congruent. But I think love comes first *logically* among these congruent attributes. This means that when speculating about God's nature, we ought to begin conceptually with love and understand the other attributes in light of love. This means that God cannot do that which is unloving. All divine attributes can be congruent, and yet one logically comes first and regulates the others.

Unfortunately, Peckham's model privileges God's sovereign will over God's love. After all, we saw that Peckham's says God "freely" and "voluntarily" decides whether to relate to and love the world. This privileges God's freedom *from* creation over relational love *for* creation. If love for creation came first logically in the divine nature, God would necessarily rather than voluntarily love us. In Peckham's view, God's will comes before love.

Similarly, if God's giving and receiving love for creation were congruent with God's sovereign will, Peckham should not insist that God is "voluntarily passible in relation to the world." The God that Peckham envisions can choose whether to love us or not, which means free choice comes before love. In Peckham's view, God's nonrelationality with the world comes

[handwritten margin note: Why is love logically first?]

logically before God's relational love for creation. Peckham logically privileges God's power over God's relational love for creatures.

The God that Peckham describes seems primarily oriented toward self-love. God "could have simply enjoyed eternal love relationship within the Trinity," says Peckham (99). In this view, relational love is eternally necessary among Trinitarian members but temporarily expressed for creatures. In other words, we can count on this God to love himself, but he may or may not love creatures. This doesn't sound like the love often expressed and commanded in the Bible! I can't think of a biblical passage to support the view that God necessarily loves himself in the Trinity but arbitrarily loves others in creation. And there are oodles of passages that say love acts for the good of the other. *But it's not arbitrary, it's covenantal*

I find Peckham's stated methodological commitment to Scripture winsome. He is a canonical theist, and I consider myself similarly committed. But the Bible doesn't explicitly support Peckham's view over mine. In fact, the Bible can't settle the issues that divide us: whether God voluntarily or essentially *relates* to creation and whether God voluntarily or essentially *loves* creation.

Peckham sprinkles in a few scriptural references to support his views on these matters. But a close reading of those passages reveals that they don't explicitly support his views and oppose mine. Besides, I could offer biblical passages to support my own view that God loves us everlastingly and necessarily (e.g., Jer 31:3, "I have loved you with an everlasting love"; Ps 136:1, "his steadfast love endures forever").

In short, I don't think the biblical canon alone can settle these issues. But I've offered numerous reasons why I think my view is better overall. I won't repeat them here, but I encourage readers to review those reasons in the longer essay I wrote for this book.

Although Peckham and I agree on so much, let me conclude by summarizing what I see as the primary differences between his view of passibility and mine. My view says God essentially relates to creation in giving and receiving love. Because God's nature includes love for creation, we can count on God always to love us. God's love is everlastingly loyal to creation, and such love is simply a part of who God is. My view says that love for us is, to use a popular phrase, "the heart of God."

he didn't create out of necessity

Peckham's view, by contrast, says God temporarily engages creation with giving and receiving love. God's nature does *not* include essential love for creation. God may or may not decide to listen, receive, empathize, or show compassion for creatures. Nothing but God's arbitrary choice prompts God to love us. God is everlastingly loyal to himself in the Trinity but not everlastingly loyal to creation. In Peckham's view, love for us is *not* the heart of God.

If the reader privileges God's freedom *from* us over God's love *for* us, she will likely find Peckham's view more attractive. But if she thinks we should privilege God's love *for us* over God's freedom *from* us, she will likely find my view more winsome.

Concluding Remarks in Defense of Qualified Passibility

JOHN C. PECKHAM

I am thankful to each of the contributors for their responses. I will respond to each one by one.

Oord claims that my view renders God's love strictly arbitrary. Unfortunately, Oord's response misrepresents and inaccurately portrays my view in numerous ways. My response to Oord's chapter already includes a rebuttal of his primary claims. In the limited space I have here, then, I will simply note some ways in which Oord's characterization of my position is misleading or flatly incorrect.

Oord falsely claims that in my view: "Nothing but God's arbitrary choice prompts God to love us." As explained at length in my work on divine love, however, I do *not* believe God's love for us can be reduced to volition. Whereas Oord thinks either God's love or will or power must have logical priority, I take God's love and will and power (and other attributes) to be equiprimordial. God's free choices are not strictly arbitrary; they are motivated by who God is.

Further, I do not think that "free choice comes before love." Rather, I believe that freedom is intrinsic to love. Again, it is Oord's view that claims God's love or will or power must be afforded logical priority, not mine.

Additionally, Oord incorrectly claims that, on my view, God might "freely decide today to give up on the creation project" and "God temporarily engages creation with giving and receiving love." However, in my view, God's engagement with creation is *not* temporary but everlasting. God has

ηⁱⁱ⁷

covenanted to maintain relationship with the world for eternity and there is no danger that God will not keep his covenantal commitment to everlasting love relationship with creation. God's "steadfast love endures forever" (Ps 136:1); God always keeps his promises and his purpose is unchanging (cf. Heb 6:17-18). Contrary to Oord's claim otherwise, then, I believe God is indeed everlastingly loyal to creation. The difference between Oord and me on this point is that Oord believes God's nature compels him to be in relation to the world; I believe God *freely* creates and maintains his steadfast love in accordance with his covenantal promises. Yes

Thus, whereas Oord thinks God has no choice but to create the world, I believe Scripture teaches that God freely and graciously chose to create this world. Here I think Oord's assumption that love *must* create is just false. Is the love of the husband and wife who do not procreate thereby deficient? I do not think so. Oord's position does not sufficiently account for supererogatory divine action, that is, God's generous action beyond the call of duty. Regarding such, God is exceedingly praiseworthy precisely in that his mercy and love *freely* exceed all obligations and reasonable expectations. As such, I think Oord's account confuses divine grace with obligation, misunderstanding God's free, generous action as obligatory.

Oord thinks Scripture does not indicate whether his view or mine is preferable, but I think Scripture does indeed teach creation *ex nihilo* (e.g., Ps 33:6; Heb 11:3) and that creation is not eternal (e.g., Col 1:16-17) and that God does not *need* this or any world (e.g., Acts 17:25) and that God's love is freely given (e.g., Hos 14:4), though not reducible to volition.

Castelo is concerned about any claim that "Scripture provides warrant for a position, such as (im)passibility, without the accompanying work of contextualizing those claims" (118). I agree with Castelo that Scripture should always be exegeted with attention to all its "contextual complexity," "cultural embeddedness," and "scandalizing particularity" (118). Yet I do not think this renders Scripture incapable of providing warrant for or against theological claims. Indeed, I think Scripture, approached in a way that carefully attends to the text in its historical and canonical context, indicates that God does indeed experience passible emotions.

Castelo also affirms what he takes to be Gavrilyuk's concern that "*language of affectivity* in God-talk (and this language in particular) has to be disciplined" and, Castelo thinks, language of "impassibility can do that work" (118). However, I think such "discipline" is far better accomplished via other terminology such as that of qualified passibility.

Dolezal's response is helpful in clarifying where our views diverge, particularly methodologically. He says I am "right to demand biblical warrant for claims about impassibility/passibility" (115). Yet he maintains that one should adopt a particular understanding of the Creator-creature distinction as a "hermeneutical principle" that "precedes Scripture and is brought to the text as a lens by which we are able to make assessments about the literal or figurative quality of the Bible's varied statements about God" (114). This particular understanding of the Creator-creature distinction presupposes as an axiom that "God is unmoved in his being."

I believe, conversely, that it is a mistake to presuppose that God is impassible as a hermeneutical principle that "precedes Scripture," instead of looking to the text for indicators regarding whether and to what extent biblical statements are figurative. In my view, doing so compromises the functional canonical authority of Scripture, even if unintentionally. How can Scripture *actually function* as "the supreme judge in all doctrinal controversies about God's nature," as Dolezal says it should, if it is not allowed to reform the interpreter's metaphysical framework? How can Scripture function as the "supreme judge" relative to the controversy over (im)passibility if Scripture itself is to be read through an axiomatic lens that presupposes God is impassible?

Dolezal and I both affirm the Creator-creature distinction, but Dolezal takes that distinction to entail divine impassibility. I do not. Indeed, I do not see any biblically warranted reason to think that the Creator of all, whose existence and essential nature indeed depends on nothing, could not open himself up to genuine, affective relationship with creation. As I understand it, qualified passibility poses no threat to divine aseity and self-sufficiency (understood to mean that God's existence and essential nature are not dependent on or derived from anything outside of himself). Rather, the kind of dependency in view in my position is only with regard to accidental properties such as God being pleased or angered by creaturely actions, which Scripture expressly and repeatedly teaches.

Regarding biblical warrant, Dolezal admits that "passages in which God is said not to change" are "underdeterminative" relative to the issue of (im)passibility, at least "taken in isolation" (115). Yet, in my view, the other passages he appeals to also do not indicate, or even support, divine impassibility. In this and other regards, I do not find the metaphysical framework on which Dolezal's argument depends to be compelling, and I think it is problematic to employ it as a lens through which Scripture is read.

Overall, I believe qualified passibility does indeed make the best sense of the biblical data; it consistently affirms the biblical testimony regarding God's passible love relationship with the world, while also affirming the biblical testimony relative to *both* divine freedom in relation to the world *and* that God is not dependent on anything else relative to his existence (aseity) or essential nature (self-sufficiency).

4

Strong Passibility

THOMAS JAY OORD

As I see it, God relates with creation. By "relate," I mean God influences creatures and creatures influence God. God is passible, to use the ancient language; God is relational, to use the contemporary term. God is affected, is vulnerable, suffers, receives, or responds to creation. God is the "most moved mover," to use Abraham Heschel and Clark Pinnock's description of divine passibility.[1]

I'm not the only person who thinks God relates with creatures. The vast majority of Christians I know think God gives and receives in relationship with creation. Most think we humans can act in ways that please or bless God. We can also anger or sadden God. And Christians aren't the only ones who think this way. Most of my Jewish and Muslim friends think God is passible, although few today use that word.[2]

Of course, sometimes what seems true turns out false. I once thought God had a body shaped like mine, except bigger. I now have reasons to think God is a universal Spirit without a localized divine body. Is what *seems* true about God being relational *actually* true?

In this essay, I explore and defend strong divine passibility or what I call God's "essential relatedness." I argue that what seems true about God being influenced by creatures *is* likely true. In fact, we have good reasons to believe divine passibility tells us something true about God's essence. It makes

---

[1]Clark H. Pinnock, *Most Moved Mover: A Theology of God's Openness* (Grand Rapids: Baker, 2001).

[2]For an example of a Jewish scholar affirming divine passibility, see Shai Held, *Abraham Joshua Heschel: The Call of Transcendence* (Bloomington: Indiana University Press, 2013). For an example of a Muslim scholar, see Farhan A. Shah, "Toward a Process-Humanistic Interpretation of Islam: An Examination of Muhammed Iqbal's God Concept" (Master's Thesis, University of Oslo, 2016).

sense to believe that creatures affect God and that God essentially relates to others.

WHAT IS POSSIBILITY?

Theologians use various words as near synonyms to passible. I've already mentioned some, but I like relational best. The fundamental claim of divine passibility is causal: creatures influence God. Creation makes an impact on God's experience. Consequently, a relational God is affected by what creatures do.

God sometimes feels emotions when influenced. God feels compassion in response to suffering, for instance, as creatures cause God to experience pity, sympathy, or empathy. Sometimes God is said to be pleased, which implies divine emotion. Sometimes God feels righteous jealousy. References to God's "wrath" are usually coupled with statements about divine anger, which is another of God's emotions. In sum, most references to divine emotions assume God engages in giving-and-receiving relationships with creation.

I'll address later the obstacles to thinking God has emotions. At present, I want to stress that questions about God's passibility or impassibility are *primarily* causal questions and secondarily about emotions. The question at stake is this: Does creation make an actual difference to God? As one who affirms a relational God and strong divine passibility, I answer that question with a resounding yes!

BIBLICAL SUPPORT FOR DIVINE PASSIBILITY

Why do so many Christians think it obvious that creation influences God? I suspect most do because they believe the Bible tells them something true about God. In fact, like me, many Christians have been reading and hearing the Bible since childhood. Scripture is a primary source of revelation, and biblical writers describe God as passible.[3]

---

[3]A host of Old Testament scholars argue in favor of divine passibility. For examples, see Walter Brueggemann, *Theology of the Old Testament: Testimony, Dispute, Advocacy* (Minneapolis: Fortress Press, 1997); Terence Fretheim, *God and the World in the Old Testament*; *The Suffering of God: An Old Testament Perspective* (Philadelphia: Fortress Press, 1984); Michael J. Chan and Brent A. Strawn, eds. *What Kind of God? Collected Essays of Terence E. Fretheim* (Winona Lake, IN: Eisenbrauns, 2015); John Goldingay, *Old Testament Theology*, vol. 1 (Downers Grove, IL: InterVarsity Press, 1993); Abraham Heschel, *The Prophets* (New York: Harper and Row, 1962). See also John Daniel Holloway work on passibility in his unpublished essay, "The Man Whom Suffering Made His Friend: Jeremiah and the Weeping God."

Listing every biblical passage depicting God as possible, engaged in give-and-receive relations, or expressing emotions would require a book—as big as a Bible! But let me offer a small sample of such verses:

- God "sees" that the created world and in which creatures "bring forth" creatures is a "good" world, even saying some are "very good" (Gen 1).

- God first considers the animals as possible companions for Adam but finds them unsuitable. So God decides to create another human (Gen 2).

- The Lord "was sorry" that he made humans, and "it grieved him to his heart" (Gen 6:6).

- God "hears" the cries of Israel and is "concerned about their suffering" (Ex 3:7 NIV).

- God hears the "groaning of the Israelites" and remembers the covenant (Ex 6:5).

- God self-identifies as a "jealous God" and "unswervingly loyal" (Ex 20:5-6 *The Message*).

- God encounters a "stiff-necked people," has anger that "burn[s]," but "relent[s]" and does not bring disaster (Ex 32:9-14 NIV).

- Being "a compassionate God," God will not "forget the covenant with your fathers" (Deut 4:31 NASB).

- The Lord foretells Hezekiah's imminent death; Hezekiah prays and asks for more time; the Lord responds by adding years to Hezekiah's life (2 Kings 20:1-7).

- God "remembered His covenant" and "relented according to the greatness of His lovingkindness" (Ps 106:45 NASB).

- "My steadfast love shall not depart from you, and my covenant of peace shall not be removed, says the LORD, who has compassion on you" (Is 54:10).

- God feels sorrow about the disaster brought on Judah (Jer 42:10).

- God is "jealous" and has "pity" on the people (Joel 2:18).

- God has "compassion" for Israel (Hos 11:8-9).

- God takes "great delight" and "rejoice[s]" (Zeph 3:17 NIV).

- God gets "extremely angry" when the nations make disasters worse (Zech 1:15).

- Mary says God helps "in remembrance of his mercy" (Lk 1:54).

- The apostle Paul warns his readers: "Do not grieve the Holy Spirit of God" (Eph 4:30), which implies that creaturely action can sadden God.

- James says, "The Lord is compassionate and merciful" (Jas 5:11).

I could list more biblical passages that point to a God whom creatures influence. Even theologians who reject divine passibility admit that biblical authors describe God as passible.

THE JESUS ARGUMENT FOR DIVINE PASSIBILITY

Christians often say that what they know best about God comes from the revelation of Jesus Christ. In Jesus, God is specially incarnated (Jn 14:9). Those who affirm divine passibility also typically believe Jesus reveals God as relational.[4]

Scripture tells us that Jesus had compassion for those in need (Mt 9:36; 14:4; 15:32; 20:34; Mk 1:41; 6:34; 8:2; Lk 7:13; 10:33). Jesus was moved by suffering and lack, and he responded with help. He experienced the pain of others as if it were his own (Mt 25:45; Acts 9:5). He showed anger in response to sin, was "troubled in spirit" when betrayed, and wept at the news of a friend's death (Mk 3:5; Jn 13:21; Jn 11:35). The writer of Hebrews says in Jesus "we do not have a high priest who is unable sympathize with our weaknesses" (Heb 4:15). In a variety of ways, Jesus was affected by others and expressed emotions in response. Jesus was passible.

Jesus teaches that God is an Abba (Father) who responds to children, and an Abba's responding is an intimately relational activity (Mk 14:36). In a story about a wayward son, Jesus describes God as a forgiving father who was "filled with compassion" for a lost son; this father "ran and put his arms around him and kissed him" (Lk 15:20). In the Sermon on the Mount, Jesus advocates

---

[4]Among the many books affirming Jesus and divine passibility, see Richard Bauckham, *Jesus and the God of Israel: God Crucified and Other Studies on the New Testament's Christology of Divine Identity* (Grand Rapids: Eerdmans, 2008); William Placher, *Narratives of a Vulnerable God: Christ, Theology, and Scripture* (Louisville: Westminster John Knox, 1994); Alan Torrance, "Does God Suffer? Incarnation and Impassibility," in *Christ in Our Place: The Humanity of God in Christ for the Reconciliation of the World*, ed. Trevor Hart (Eugene, OR: Wipf and Stock, 1989).

imitating God: "Be compassionate just as your Father is compassionate" (Lk 6:36 CEB). I could cite more examples of Jesus describing God as relational.

Perhaps more effectively than any theologian in the past half-century, Jürgen Moltmann has argued that Jesus' death on the cross points to God's passibility. In Jesus, God identifies with the godless and godforsaken. The cross reveals that suffering is internal to trinitarian life, says Moltmann. The crucified God shares in the suffering of the world, and thereby shows solidarity with those who suffer.[5] In short, Jesus' suffering on the cross reveals that God suffers.

It could be argued, however, that the passibility of Jesus—whom many Christians call the "God-human"—describes only his humanity. Perhaps Jesus' deity remained impassible. This argument might prompt us to ask, Should we project onto God the relationality we see in Jesus? Are Christians engaging in anthropopathic projection when they say Jesus reveals God as passible and capable of expressing emotions?[6]

When answering these questions, we should begin by admitting that although Jesus represents God's character (Heb 1:3; 1 Jn 3:16), he did not re-present every divine attribute. Jesus was neither omniscient nor omnipresent, for instance. And yet, Christians think God is like Jesus in important ways. If Jesus was affected by others, expressed emotions, and yet remained steadfastly loving, there are strong christological grounds for thinking God can do the same.

Instead of worrying that we might be projecting Jesus' passible and emotion-laded attributes onto God, we should believe we are engaging in a theopathic exercise that projects God's passibility and emotions onto Jesus. The compassionate God, for instance, is revealed in the compassionate Jesus. And when we who are "conformed to the image of his Son" express positive relations and appropriate emotions, we imitate the passible and emotional God (Rom 8:29). Perhaps this is part of what it means to be made in God's image (Gen 1:26).

In sum, Christians have strong christological arguments to support divine passibility. When Jesus relates with others, expresses emotions, feels compassion, and suffers on the cross, he is acting like God.

---

[5]Jürgen Moltmann, *The Crucified God: The Cross of Christ As the Foundation and Criticism of Christian Theology* (London: SCM, 1974, 2001).
[6]Marcel Sarot explores this in *God, Passibility, and Corporeality* (Leuven: Peeters, 1992).

THE THEO-LOGIC OF LOVE

I want to draw together what I have said thus far to make a broader argument for why we should believe God is relational/passible. That argument might be called "the theo-logic of love." The love described in Scripture, in Jesus, and in our own best experiences indicates that expressions of love are partly shaped by responses to others. An entirely unrelated, unresponsive, and isolated person—if such a being existed—would not love. Love requires relationships of giving-and-receiving influence.

One of the biggest errors committed by Christian theologians of yesteryear was to think God's love involves only outgoing benevolence with no receptive relationality. Many wrongly thought God's love only gives and never receives. Let me offer a few examples of this erroneous thinking.

Thomas Aquinas thought God acted benevolently toward creatures but was not affected by creaturely love. "A relation of God to creatures is not a reality in God," he writes. God knows creatures as ideas without being causally affected by them.[7] Influencing relations with creation "are not really in Him," Aquinas says, and "are ascribed to him only in our understanding."[8] In other words, we only *imagine* God gives and receives in loving relationship. But in reality, God does not. If Aquinas is right, biblical statements about God's compassion are fictional. Creatures cannot bless God. And God never responds to sin by offering forgiveness.

Anselm made the same error. "How are you compassionate, and at the same time passionless?" Anselm asks rhetorically. "For if you are passionless, you do not feel sympathy. And if you do not feel sympathy, your heart is not wretched from sympathy for the wretched. But this it is to be compassionate." In response to his own question, Anselm offers the answer we saw in Aquinas: "When you behold us in our wretchedness, we experience the effect of compassion, but you do not experience the feeling. Therefore, you are both compassionate, because you do save the wretched and spare those who sin against you, and not compassionate, because you are affected by no

---

[7]Thomas Aquinas, *Summa theologiae: Complete English Edition in Five Volumes,* translated by the Fathers of the English Dominican Province (Westminster, MD: Christian Classics, 1981), I.6.2, ad 1.
[8]Thomas Aquinas, *Summa contra gentiles* (Notre Dame, IN: University of Notre Dame Press, 1981), II.13-14.

sympathy for wretchedness."[9] We *think* God is compassionate, according to Anselm, when God is actually not.

In contrast to Aquinas and Anselm, I think God's love involves more than outgoing benevolence. God's love also involves incoming empathy, receiving, and sometimes suffering. And I stand with many other theologians who affirm divine possibility.[10] God's love requires both giving and receiving. And God is *actually* compassionate, not just apparently so.

The theo-logic of love in Scripture points to God's love as relationally full orbed rather than one dimensional. For instance, God expresses the *agapē* form of love by responding to sin with forgiveness and healing—activities that assume passibility. God repays evil with good, and we should do likewise (Lk 6:27-31; Rom 12:21; 1 Thess 5:15; 1 Pet 3:9). God's *agapē* promotes overall wellbeing by responding to activity that promotes ill-being.[11] I call divine *agapē* "in spite of" love, and it requires divine passibility.

Scripture tells us that God expresses giving-and-receiving *philia* love with creatures (Ex 33:12; 2 Chron 20:7; Is 41:8; Jas 2:2, 23; 2 Tim 3:2;

---

[9]St. Anselm, *Proslogium*, trans. Sidney Norton Deane (La Salle, IL, 1951), 13-14.

[10]Among the many theologians who argue that God is passible, see especially Dietrich Bonhoeffer, *The Cost of Discipleship* (New York: Macmillan, 1949); Gregory A. Boyd, *Is God to Blame? Beyond Pat Answers to the Problem of Suffering* (Downers Grove, IL: InterVarsity Press, 2003); John B. Cobb Jr., *God and the World* (Philadelphia: Westminster, 1969); Isaak August Dorner, "The History of the Doctrine of the Immutability of God," in *Divine Immutability*, trans. Robert R. Williams and Claude Welch (Minneapolis: Fortress Press, 1994), 82-130; H. Ray Dunning, *Grace, Faith, and Holiness* (Kansas City, MO; Beacon Hill, 1988); Paul Fiddes, *The Creative Suffering of God* (New York: Oxford University Press, 1988); Catherine Keller, *From a Broken Web: Separation, Sexism and Self* (Boston: Beacon, 1986); Kazoh Kitamori, *Theology of the Pain of God*, 5th ed. (Richmond, VA: John Knox Press, 1965); Jung Young Lee, *God Suffers for Us* (Netherlands: Martinus Nijhoff, The Hague, 1974); Bruce McCormack, "Divine Impassibility or Simply Divine Constancy: Implications for Karl Barth's Later Christology for Debates over Impassibility," in *Divine Impassibility and the Mystery of Human Suffering*, ed. James F. Keating and Thomas Joseph White (Grand Rapids: Eerdmans, 2009); Jürgen Moltmann, *Crucified God*; Thomas Jay Oord, *The Nature of Love: A Theology* (St. Louis, MO: Chalice, 2010), Clark Pinnock, *Most Moved Mover*; Pinnock et al., *The Openness of God: A Biblical Challenge to the Traditional Understand of God* (Downers Grove, IL: InterVarsity Press, 1994); Jeff Pool, *God's Wounds: Hermeneutic of the Christian Symbol of Divine Suffering*, vol. 1: *Divine Vulnerability and Creation* (Cambridge: James Clarke and Co., 2009); John Sanders, *The God Who Risks: A Theology of Divine Providence* (Downers Grove, IL: IVP Academic, 2007); T. F. Torrance, *The Christian Doctrine of God* (New York: Continuum, 1996); Daniel Day Williams, "Suffering and Being in Empirical Theology," in *The Future of Empirical Theology*, ed. B. L. Meland (Chicago: University of Chicago Press, 1969), 175-94; Nicholas Wolterstorff, "Suffering Love," in *Philosophy and the Christian Faith*, ed. Thomas V. Morris (Notre Dame, IN: University of Notre Dame Press, 1990).

[11]I provide a precise definition of love, *agapē, eros,* and *philia,* in Thomas Jay Oord, *Defining Love: A Philosophical, Scientific, and Theological Engagement* (Grand Rapids: Brazos, 2010).

Titus 3:4). Because God is passible, God enjoys friendships and engages in relational covenants. As the psalmist puts it, "The friendship of the LORD is for those who fear him, / and he makes his covenant known to them" (Ps 25:14). God's *philia* promotes overall wellbeing by relating to creatures in companionship, bonds of alliance, and other relationships. I call divine *philia* "alongside of" love, and it requires divine passibility.

God's passibility is evident in divine *eros* as God evaluates and values creation (2 Tim 4:8; Jn 12:43; Heb 1:9). God sees that creation is good (Gen 1) and responds with pleasure. God loves the world so much that He gives the only begotten Son so that those who believe might have eternal life (Jn 3:16). God's *eros* promotes overall wellbeing by appreciating and enhancing what is valuable. I call divine *eros* "because of" love, and it requires divine passibility.

In sum, God's full-orbed love requires not just God's giving. It also requires God's receiving. That's the theo-logic of divine love.[12]

A RELATIONAL GOD CHANGES?

The idea that God relates with others fits nicely with the idea that God's experience changes. God's moment-by-moment life is "mutable," to use classical language, rather than immutable. Because God receives from creatures, creatures change the state of God's experience moment by moment. Being the most moved mover, we might say, also means God is on the move.

God's experience changes when creatures affect God. It makes no sense to say God's emotions change from tranquility to anger or from delight to disappointment if there were not a "before" and "after" in God's experience. In fact, what creatures do sometimes leads God to have a change of mind. More than forty biblical passages say God "repents" (*nāḥam*), which means God changes plans.[13] Divine passibility and divine mutability are closely associated.

I find it impossible to make sense of basic Christian claims about God as Creator, redeemer, Savior, forgiver, and so on, if God's experience does not change. The creation of our universe, for instance, suggests a before and after in God's creating. God as redeemer and Savior suggests times in God's

---

[12]I have made an extensive argument for full-orbed divine love as involving *agapē, eros,* and *philia* in Oord, *Nature of Love.*

[13]On Old Testament statements about God repenting, see Fretheim, *Suffering of God,* and Chan and Strawn, *What Kind of God?,* chap. 2. See also R. W. L. Moberly, *Old Testament Theology: Reading the Hebrew Bible as Christian Scripture* (Grand Rapids: Baker Academic, 2013), chap. 4.

experience before this redeeming and saving. Forgiving a particular sin involves a change in God's experience: at one moment, the sin was not committed and therefore not in need of forgiveness. Later the sin occurred and God forgave. Central Christian claims only make sense if God's experiential states change from one to another.[14] God's moment-by-moment experience must be mutable.

Most theologians who affirm divine impassibility and immutability also entertain a particular notion of God's perfection.[15] The perfect one cannot change, they think, because this would mean the changed one was not previously perfect. Or it would mean the changed one moved from perfection to imperfection. Carl F. H. Henry puts it this way: "God is perfect and, if imperfect, can only change for the worse."[16] Augustine spells out what this means: "There is no modification in God, because there is nothing in him that can be changed or lost . . . he remains absolutely unchangeable."[17]

Augustine and Henry rely on a stunted view of perfection. Their view fails to account for the possibility that God can change perfectly. In fact, many theologians fail to consider the possibility that God can be perfectly unchanging in some respects and perfectly changing in others.[18]

The psalmist points to both forms of divine perfection: God "relented according to the abundance of his steadfast love" (Ps 106:45 ESV). To relent means to change; steadfast means to change not. God's love involves both forms of perfection: perfect flexibility and perfect stability.

This wider view of perfection came to my mind recently while worshiping. I joined the congregation in singing these lines from a worship song made popular by Chris Tomlin:

---

[14]R. T. Mullins makes this point strongly as a criticism of the "timeless God" in *The End of the Timeless God* (New York: Oxford University Press, 2016).

[15]R. T. Mullins also does admirable work describing the problems that arise when thinking God is in all ways impassible in *The End of the Timeless God*. See also Charles Hartshorne, *The Divine Relativity* (New Haven, CT: Yale University Press, 1948).

[16]Carl F. H. Henry, *God, Revelation, and Authority: The God Who Stands and Stays*, part 1, vol. 5 (Waco, TX: Word, 1982), 304. For another who endorses the argument that God cannot change in any sense, see Stephen Charnock in *God Without Passions: A Reader*, ed. Samuel Renihan (Palmdale, CA: Reformed Baptist Academic Press, 2015), 144-54.

[17]Augustine, *The Trinity*, Works of Saint Augustine, vol. 5, ed. John E. Rotelle, trans. Edmund Hill (New York: New City Press, 2012).

[18]Charles Hartshorne should be given credit for being one of the first thinkers to articulate this expanded view of divine perfection. Among his many books, see *Man's Vision of God and the Logic of Theism* (Chicago and New York: Willett, Clark, and Co., 1941), 348.

> You're a good, good Father;
>
> It's who you are, who you are . . .
>
> You are perfect in all of your ways[19]

The God that Augustine and Henry imagine is perfect in some ways but not others. The God of strong divine passibility is perfect in all ways. I'll explain this later in the essay.

THREE WAYS PASSIBILITY MATTERS

Some readers may wonder if questions about God's passibility are merely theoretical. Some may think reflection on the meaning of passibility an abstract exercise not connected to everyday living. So let me briefly note three ways it matters that we affirm divine passibility.

Throughout Scripture we find examples of believers petitioning God in prayer. God sometimes even invites petitions: "Ask of me, and I will make the nations your heritage, / the ends of the earth your possession" (Ps 2:8). Jesus says, "If you ask anything of the Father in my name, he will give it to you" (Jn 16:23). We find examples of petitionary prayer throughout Scripture, and most Christians today at least sometimes ask God to do something.

If God is impassible and creatures cannot make a difference to what God does, why pray petitionary prayers? Why ask God to do something or help in some way? Petitioning prayer presupposes that our requests affect God and that God may act differently. But if God is unaffected by what we do, it makes no sense to petition God.

In the name of petitionary prayer, therefore, we should affirm divine passibility.

We should also affirm divine passibility as the basis for God's empathetic love. We all suffer, and some people suffer deeply. Oppression can be physical, emotional, social, racial, gender based, sexual, spiritual, political, or something else. Biblical writers describe God as empathizing with the oppressed. God cares, consoles those in pain, and has compassion. And God calls on believers to comfort those who suffer. The apostle Paul describes God's empathetic love this way:

---

[19]Tony Brown and Pat Barrett, "Good, Good Father," recorded by Chris Tomlin on *Never Lose Sight* (Atlanta: Sixsteps, 2016).

Blessed be the God and Father of our Lord Jesus Christ, the Father of mercies and the God of all consolation, who consoles us in all our affliction, so that we may be able to console those who are in any affliction with the consolation with which we ourselves are consoled by God. For just as the sufferings of Christ are abundant for us, so also our consolation is abundant through Christ. (2 Cor 1:3-5)

It's hard to feel comforted by those who never experience anything remotely like our suffering. The unaffected can't relate to what we're feeling. The impassible God *never* suffers and never relates! As Aquinas and Anselm argue, the impassible God does not empathize. Consequently, the impassible God cannot comfort others from the perspective of one who has been affected negatively.

By contrast, the passible God *is* empathetic. The relational God of love is a fellow sufferer who empathetically understands our suffering.[20] Oppressed creatures can feel comforted by a passible One who is "the God of all comfort" (NIV).[21]

For the sake of we who are oppressed, therefore, we should affirm divine passibility.

A third reason we should affirm God's passibility pertains to following biblical commands to act like God. The apostle Paul writes these powerful words: "Be imitators of God, as beloved children, and live in love" (Eph 5:1-2). Paul also tells his readers to "be kind to one another, tenderhearted, forgiving one another, as God in Christ has forgiven you" (Eph 4:32). Elsewhere in Scripture people are instructed to be holy as God is holy (1 Pet 1:14-16) and Jesus says we should imitate God's compassion by being compassionate (Lk 6:36 CEB).

It's difficult to imagine how we can imitate an impassible God in these ways. Compassion, for instance, requires being affected by those in need because it means to "suffer with." Is it possible to express nonempathetic and nonemotional compassion? No. In fact, I have no idea what nonempathetic compassion would mean! But we *can* imitate the compassion of

---

[20]Alfred North Whitehead famously called God the "fellow sufferer who understands" in *Process and Reality: An Essay in Cosmology*, ed. David Ray Griffin and Donald W. Sherburne (New York: Free Press, 1978, 1929), 351.

[21]I could list *numerous* books arguing that the oppressed can find comfort in a passible God. But as one example, see James Cone, *God of the Oppressed*, rev. ed. (Maryknoll, NY: Orbis, 1997).

a God who is passible. And with God's help, we can fulfill the call to imitate God's love that we find in Scripture.[22]

In the name of imitating a loving God, therefore, we should affirm divine passibility.

DOES GOD HAVE EMOTIONS?

I've mentioned God's emotions already, but I want to address that subject a little more. Some Christians believe God has no emotions. They believe this in part because they think only embodied beings express emotion. "Every passion of the appetite takes place through some bodily change," said Aquinas about emotions. "None of this can take place in God, since He is not a body."[23]

I agree with Christians who say God is bodiless or incorporeal. I think there are strong biblical grounds to say God is an omnipresent spirit. While I do think God is incarnate in the world, I don't think God has a localized divine body. Like most people, I think biblical stories that speak of an embodied God use anthropomorphic language. The dominant biblical descriptions refer to God as bodiless: *ruah, pneuma*, spirit, mind, soul, word, or wind.

So are Aquinas and others right? Are only embodied beings capable of emotion? I don't see how Aquinas or anyone else could demonstrate that a disembodied God cannot feel emotion. None of us knows what it's like to be disembodied, so we can't know that emotions require a body. Besides, the argument that God was specially incarnated in Jesus, as I discussed above, supports the view that an essentially bodiless God feels emotion.

Many Christians in yesteryear worried that emotions undermine reason because emotions can be volatile. Greek gods and unscrupulous humans sometimes engaged in emotional outbursts that produced immoral behavior. Many early Christians, consequently, claimed that a perfectly moral God would not feel or express emotions. God is emotionless (*apatheia*), they said, despite ample scriptural witness to the contrary.

In contrast to those who believe God feels no emotion, I believe God feels emotion and acts on those feelings. But we need to make two

---

[22]See Roberto Sirvent for a lengthy argument for the cogency of *imitatio Dei* and divine passibility in *Embracing Vulnerability: Human and Divine* (Eugene, OR: Pickwick, 2014).
[23]Aquinas, *Summa contra gentiles* I.89.3.

qualifications to this belief to overcome legitimate concerns about divine emotions.

The first legitimate concern is that God expresses emotions using a divine body. Biblical writers might say, for instance, that God's eyes cry tears when feeling sad. They might say God's face shines in happiness. Or they might say God's anger is red hot. As I've already noted, I don't think God has a localized divine body. But we can believe God feels the emotions of sadness, anger, and happiness without also thinking God has actual eyes that cry, an actual face that shines, or an actual body that gets hot. We should believe, in other words, that biblical writers use bodily metaphors to describe God expressing emotions. Divine emotions can be real even if references to God's body parts are metaphorical.

The second legitimate worry to overcome is the view that God's emotions might lead God to act irrationally or immorally. To overcome this worry, we should say God's unchanging nature makes it possible for God to feel and express emotions without becoming irrational or immoral. God feels and expresses emotions in accordance with God's wise and good nature. By contrast, we don't have unchangingly good and wise natures. Unlike God, we creatures sometimes feel emotions and respond irrationally or immorally.[24]

The appeal to God's unchanging nature and my comments about God's perfections lead naturally to considering how to incorporate positive elements of impassibility while rejecting unhelpful elements.

INCORPORATING THE STRENGTHS OF IMPASSIBILITY WITHOUT ITS WEAKNESSES

Few theological views are *entirely* false. Smart and loving people usually have good reasons for promoting their theological perspectives, even if we don't think such perspectives are helpful overall.[25] In this section, I

---

[24]On this, see also Ryan Mullins, "Impassibility, Omnisubjectivity, and the Problem of Unity in Love," in Oliver D. Crisp, James Arcadi, and Jordan Wessling, eds., *Love, Human and Divine: Contemporary Essays in Systematic and Philosophical Theology* (New York: Bloomsbury, 2019); Anastasia Philippa Scrutton, *Thinking Through Feeling: God, Emotion and Passibility* (New York: Continuum International Publishing Group, 2011); and Charles Taliaferro, "The Passibility of God," *Religious Studies* 25 (1989).

[25]I thank Eric Silverman for providing me with his defense of impassibility, although I do not fully affirm it. See "Impassibility and Divine Love," in *Models of God and Alternative Ultimate Realities*, ed. Jeanine Diller and Asa Kasher (New York: Springer, 2013). Silverman is an example of a wise and good person with whom I disagree on the issue of God's passibility.

incorporate the strengths of divine impassibility while rejecting the view's weaknesses.

In one respect, those who say God is impassible and immutable are right: God's *nature* is impassible and immutable. When Malachi and James quote God saying, "I the LORD do not change" (Mal 3:6; Jas 1:17), they refer to God's immutable nature. God's essence is unchanging and unaffected by creation. But in another respect, as I have been arguing, God is passible and mutable. God's actual *experience* is passible and mutable. As the living Lord of history, God's experience changes when affected by creatures. A personal God lovingly relates to others in giving-and-receiving relationships.

Saying God's nature is impassible but God's experience is passible helps us make sense of otherwise puzzling biblical passages. In 1 Samuel, for instance, the author says the Lord "is not a man, that he should repent" (1 Sam 15:29 KJV). This statement highlights God's impassible and immutable nature. Soon after, however, the same author says, "The LORD repented that he had made Saul king over Israel" (1 Sam 15:35 KJV). This statement highlights God's passible and mutable experience: God sees what occurred and, in the name of love, changes course. God does not repent in one sense but does in another.

Or take a biblical passage I've often sung:

The steadfast love of the LORD never ceases,
    his mercies never come to an end;
they are new every morning;
    great is your faithfulness. (Lam 3:22-23)

This passage emphasizes God's nature of love as unchangingly steadfast and everlasting. But it also says God's expressions of love change: they are new every moment.

Some call the idea that God's nature is impassible while God's experience is passible "dipolar" theism. Alfred North Whitehead, for instance, said God has two "poles" or "natures": primordial and consequential.[26] While no language is perfect, I find it confusing to say God has two natures or two poles. I prefer to say God's immaterial nature is impassible and God's actual

---

[26]See the writings of Daniel Dombrowski, David Ray Griffin, Charles Hartshorne, Donald Viney, and Alfred North Whitehead for various versions and meanings of dipolar theism.

experience is passible; God's immaterial nature is immutable and God's actual experience is mutable. But I agree with the general point of divine dipolarity: we are wise to distinguish between God's abstract essence and God's relational experience.

Most theologians affirm that God is similar to creatures in some respects but differs in other respects. They often couch these similarities and differences in the language of divine transcendence and immanence. Or they talk about doing theology *via negativa* and *via positiva*. Or theologians refer to apophatism and anthropomorphism.

Thinking God is in *all* ways different from us leads to absolute mystery. Appealing to such mystery is a problem for Christian witness, because absolute apophatism is unthinkable. Believing God is in *all* ways similar to us also has problems, however. In this view, God is simply another version of ourselves. Absolute anthropomorphism makes God in our image.

Saying that God has an impassible nature but relational experience helps us affirm both divine transcendence and immanence. God transcends creatures by having an eternal, unchanging, and unaffected nature. God is different. But God's experience is analogous to creaturely experience, because it is sequential, changing, and involves giving-and-receiving relationships.

Affirming similarities and differences between the Creator and creatures is vital to make sense of love. We can trust that God *always* loves, because love is an essential attribute of God's nature. That's divine transcendence. Creatures don't have eternal natures in which love is essential. But *how* God loves varies from moment to moment, depending on what's best for creation. In some moments God loves by calling creatures to repent; other times God loves by encouraging creatures to persevere in doing good; other times God loves by consoling, teaching, or inviting us to join in the work of salvation. In choosing how to express love in any moment, God is not entirely different from creatures. That's divine immanence. We reflect being created in God's image when we choose to love in sequential, changing, and giving-and-receiving ways.

In sum, the traditional view of impassibility points to an important way God is different: God has an immutable and impassible nature. God is perfect in this way. But impassibility fails to affirm how God is similar to creatures. It fails to describe how God is affected by others and how God's experience changes in relationship. We should believe God is perfectly possible too.

THE GOD BEHIND THE CURTAIN?

Most of what I've said thus far could be affirmed by anyone who thinks God is passible. I promised earlier, however, to defend what the editors of this book call "strong passibility." Strong divine passibility doesn't say God is affected or changes in *all* respects. Strong passibility also doesn't portray God as changing in all respects. God's nature is impassible and immutable, as I have explained, but God's living experience is passable and mutable.

Some Christians think fallible creatures like us should not speculate that God is strongly passible. They admit the evidence from Scripture, creaturely experience, and the theo-logic of love points to a passible God. But saying God is strongly passible or essentially relational is to claim something about who God is and not merely about how God is revealed. "Who are we to know whether God essentially relates with others?" they ask. "We should not speculate about who God truly is."

I understand this worry. Let me be quick to respond that I don't have secret information about God's essence. I don't *know* that God is essentially relational, in the sense of being certain of this truth. And some questions probably don't deserve spending much time trying to answer. No need to debate how many angels can dance on the head of a pin.

But Christians have good reasons to speculate about who God truly is. And we have good reasons to claim, in humility, that God is strongly passible. If God is loving and if love involves real relations, it's important to make some sense of God's giving-and-receiving love. Speculating about God is normal and important.

A scene from *The Wizard of Oz* comes to mind when I hear someone say we should only do constructive theology from what God has revealed and not speculate about who God truly is. When Dorothy and the crew encountered the Great Oz, they heard a booming voice, saw smoke, and trembled in the mystery they encountered. They imagined a deity with various attributes. It turned out, however, that the revelation did not accurately portray the revealer. An ordinary man was the source of what appeared divine. A fabricated revelation deceived Dorothy and the crew.

I think God is different from the man behind the curtain. God is not a deceiver. Consequently, we have good reasons to believe that how God self-reveals corresponds with who God truly is. Believers have grounds to speculate that the picture of God painted in Jesus, Scripture, and other sources of revelation—One who is lovingly relational—tells us something true about God's nature. In the case of passibility, we should believe that engaging in giving-and-receiving relationships is an essential attribute of God.

I'm not saying we can fully understand the revelation. And I'm not saying our perceptive capacities are flawless. But I am saying it's normal to speculate about what God is truly like. And I'm saying we have sources and evidence to guide our speculating. After all, it's just as speculative to say God *does not* essentially relate to others as to say God *does*. Advocates of weak and strong passibility are equally speculative in other words. And those who argue against *any* speculating about God are often the first to criticize statements they think inaccurate. In doing so, they show their implicit speculations about God.[27]

The God revealed as passible is also the God behind the curtain. We have good grounds to speculate that God is strongly passible and essentially relates to others.

STRONG PASSIBILITY, THE TRINITY, AND THEOCOSMOCENTRISM

The strong divine passibility view I defend says being affected by others is a necessary attribute of God's nature. God doesn't voluntarily choose to be affected; God is necessarily affected. I have been using the phrase "essentially relational" to describe strong divine passibility.

I take the biblical phrase, "God is love," to mean that love is an essential divine attribute. If God is essentially loving and love always involves relational giving and receiving, God must be essentially relational. Strong divine passibility says God is necessarily and everlastingly passible.

There are two ways (and a third that combines them) to affirm strong divine passibility. The first says God essentially relates in Godself. This view is typically associated with a vision of God as a social Trinity. The Father, Son, and Holy Spirit (or other names we might use) have everlastingly related with one another. Some call this relating a perichoretic dance. This trinitarian view affirms that God everlastingly and necessarily relates in Godself.

---

[27]I'm grateful to Jeff Pool for our conversations on these issues.

There are several downsides to placing all one's emphasis on the Trinity to affirm strong passibility. One downside is that saying divine persons relate to one another sounds to many people like tritheism rather than mono-theism. Real relations require real differences; real relations among persons require more than one person. Few Christians want to say that three Gods exist.

Those who affirm the social Trinity also typically affirm the idea that God once existed alone and then created the universe out of nothing. They say God necessarily loves and relates in Trinity but contingently loves and re-lates with creation. The downside of this view, however, is that God's love for creation is arbitrary in the sense that there is no essential divine attribute for love of creaturely others. God by nature does not love nondivine others.

[margin note: Problem here — non-divine others once did not exist.]

The view that God only loves necessarily within the Trinity can also sound like God is inherently selfish. After all, God necessarily loves Godself and contingently loves creatures. By contrast, many believe love promotes the wellbeing of those beyond the lover. And imitating God involves loving others not just ourselves. *[margin note: But God does love others!]*

Those who affirm God as essentially related in Trinity respond to these criticisms. The most common response says it's a mystery how God can be both one and essentially self-related as three. Some regard this as the highest of holy mysteries. And we should simply believe God will always love crea-tures, despite there being no love-for-creation attribute essential to God's nature.

The second way to affirm that God essentially relates with others says God essentially relates with creatures. This way denies that God once existed alone and at some time decided to create the universe out of nothing. In-stead, God always and necessarily relates with creatures, because God always creates others with whom God relates.

I call this view theocosmocentrism, but some forms of panentheism also affirm it.[28] Theocosmocentrism says we make the best sense of reality if we refer both to God and creation. The strong passibility version of

---

[28]Panentheism can be conceived as God being necessarily or contingently related to creation. For an example of panentheism's variety of meanings, see Philip Clayton and Arthur Peacocke, eds., *In Whom We Live and Move and Have Our Being: Panentheistic Reflections on God's Presence in a Scientific World* (Grand Rapids: Eerdmans, 2004).

theocosmocentrism says God necessarily loves and relates to creation, but the particular ways God loves and relates are contingent.[29]

One disadvantage to the theocosmocentric way of affirming strong divine passibility is that many people cannot fathom how God everlastingly relates to creation. Most Christians accept that God had no beginning, although they cannot fathom that view. They also accept a big-bang cosmology that says our universe had a beginning. So they cannot fathom how God *everlastingly* creates and relates to creation. Affirming both requires believing God was creating before the big bang.[30] That's difficult for many to conceive.

Another downside to the idea that God always relates to creatures (at least in the minds of some) is that the idea isn't explicitly trinitarian. Some theologians want to keep the Trinity front and center.[31] Saying God essentially relates to creatures doesn't require belief in Trinity, at least not obviously so.

But this downside can be overcome. One can affirm that God essentially relates in Trinity *and* that God essentially relates with creatures. Both types of necessary relations can be true simultaneously. We might even consider Jesus' revelation of a relational God as evidence of this doubly essential divine relatedness.[32]

To conclude, let me note that one could affirm any of these versions of strong divine passibility and think God exists necessarily. Strong passibility and divine aseity are compatible. God can necessarily exist and essentially relate to divine others or creaturely others or both. There is no logical contradiction. The steadfast love of the Lord can literally endure forever—whether in Trinity, toward creation, or both (Ps 118).

---

[29]See Oord, *Nature of Love*, 147.

[30]For essays exploring how God is Creator but does not create out of nothing, see Thomas Jay Oord, ed. *Theologies of Creation: Ex Nihilo and Its New Rivals* (New York: Routledge, 2014). I argue for a view of creation that says God always creates in love out of that which God previously created, and God's creating has been going on everlastingly.

[31]See, for instance, Kevin Vanhoozer's emphasis on the Trinity's primacy as he engages my theology of love in "Love Without Measure? John Webster's Unfinished Dogmatic Account of the Love of God, in Dialogue with Thomas Jay Oord's Interdisciplinary Theological Account," *International Journal of Systematic Theology* 19:4 (October 2017): 505-26. My response to Vanhoozer will appear in a book of essays edited by Jordan Wessling.

[32]I explore doubly necessary divine relations in Oord, *Nature of Love*. For an argument focused on Jesus as the key insight for such double necessity, see Jürgen Moltmann, *The Trinity and the Kingdom: The Doctrine of God* (Philadelphia: Fortress, 1993).

WHY IT MATTERS TO AFFIRM STRONG PASSIBILITY

So what? Earlier in this essay, I noted reasons why we should affirm God's passibility. One might now ask: Does it matter that we affirm the *strong* version of divine passibility? After all, biblical writers don't explicitly endorse one version of passibility instead of the other.

I've already provided one reason why it matters: we should unite conceptually how God self-reveals with who God truly is. The God witnessed to in Jesus, the Bible, and in other forms of revelation is the God behind the curtain. Strong passibility provides the only option offered in this book to make the claim that the passible God revealed is essentially relational.

But let me add four more reasons we should affirm strong divine passibility.

First, affirming strong passibility provides a consistent view of divine love. If love is an essential divine attribute and God essentially and everlastingly expresses love in relations with others, strong divine passibility makes sense. Strong divine passibility does not force us to do apophatic gymnastics when speaking of God's love. It doesn't balk at speculating about God's nature. Strong divine passibility provides a coherent framework for conceiving of God's love.

To affirm that love is an essential attribute in God, we should affirm strong divine passibility.

Second, if God's love is essentially relational and God necessarily relates with creatures (theocosmocentrism), we have assurance that God always loves us. God loves us no matter what, because that's the kind of being God is. Weak divine passibility cannot affirm this, because it says God's love for us is contingent. The weak view cannot say God necessarily loves creation. And those who deny divine passibility altogether cannot speak coherently about God being compassionate or expressing love in giving-and-receiving relations.

To affirm unambiguously God's steadfast love for us, we should affirm strong divine passibility.

Third, I've argued in other publications that God's love is uncontrolling. Strong divine passibility fits nicely with the view that God's love is *necessarily* uncontrolling, because divine love necessarily gives and receives. Believing God cannot control others solves the central issue in the problem of evil: the God who cannot control is not culpable for failing to prevent evil.

I call this "essential kenosis."[33] Although one could affirm weak divine passibility and the uncontrolling love of God, the strong divine passibility view fits uncontrolling love better.

To affirm clearly that God is not culpable for evil, we should affirm strong divine passibility.

Finally, the theocosmocentric version of strong divine passibility provides grounds for believing it is *necessarily* true that God will "never leave you or forsake you" (Heb 13:5; Deut 31:6). The other views in this book cannot affirm that God necessarily relates to creatures. If those views are correct, God may choose to leave us and forsake us. There's nothing to prevent God from giving up and abandoning us. Those views provide no confidence God will always be with us. False - his covenant love endures

To be confident that God will never leave us or forsake us, we should affirm strong divine passibility.

THREE DIAGNOSTIC QUESTIONS

I want to demonstrate that you, the reader, probably affirm strong divine passibility without knowing it. To do this, please answer the following three questions honestly. Answer in your head before reading my responses.

Do you think God *could* ever leave us, forsake us, or stop loving us?

Most people answer yes. They think it's *possible* for God to choose to be unrelated, unaffected, and uninfluenced. In their view, God *could* choose to leave us and forsake us. God *could* choose to stop loving us. "God sovereignly chooses to love the world," they might say. This is the weak passibility view, and it's probably the stated (but not actual) view of most Christians I know.

Let's move to the second question: Do you think God *would* ever leave us, forsake us, or stop loving us?

Most people answer no. They think God will always relate with us, always be present to us, always love, and always support us. In their view, we can trust God in these crucial ways.

---

[33]See my arguments in *The Uncontrolling Love of God: An Open and Relational Theory of Providence* (Downers Grove, IL: IVP Academic, 2015) and various essays in *Uncontrolling Love: Essays Exploring the Uncontrolling Love of God, with Introductory Essays by Thomas Jay Oord,* ed. Chris Baker et al. (San Diego, CA: SacraSage, 2017).

Those who think God *could* stop loving us, however, have no good reasons to think God *would not* stop loving. Those who think God *could* leave us and forsake us have no good reasons to think God *would never* choose to leave us or forsake us. There is no justification for such views.

Let me put it another way, if God's eternal nature does not include love for creation, we have no good reason to think God will always be with us and never forsake us. And if God's eternal nature does not include love for creation, there's no good reason to think God will continue loving us in a give-and-receive relationship.

And that leads to the third question: *Why* do you think God would never leave us, never forsake us, or never stop loving us?

Most people answer this question, "that's just who God is." They say, "If God left us, forsook us, or stopped loving us, God wouldn't be acting like God." Or they offer a variation of these answers. When answering this third, "why," question, most people appeal to their deep belief about who God truly is.

This deeper belief shows that people really *do* think God is essentially relational. Although they may not articulate it well, most think God's love for us is an essential aspect of what it means to be God. Saying "that's just who God is" is really saying, "It's God's nature to be like that." God can't help but love us because that's God's nature.

Those who believe God by nature loves creation affirm strong divine passibility, even if they can't articulate this belief well.

STRONG DIVINE PASSIBILITY IS LIKELY TRUE

As I close, I return to a claim I made at the outset. I said that what seems true about God being influenced by creatures *is* likely true. In light of my recent arguments, I'll also add that strong divine passibility is likely true.

It's important to me that I add the word "likely" to these claims. I don't have God figured out. I'm not certain about the truth of my statements. I see as if looking through a darkened glass (1 Cor 13:12 KJV), so I don't know beyond a shadow of a doubt that God is strongly passible.

I find strong divine passibility more plausible, however, than the other views described in this book. As I have pointed out, there are better reasons to think God is strongly passible than weakly passible or not passible at all. It makes most sense to say God is essentially relational.

So in humility, I offer my arguments to give an account of the hope that is within me (1 Pet 3:15). And because I believe in strong divine passibility, I believe my offerings make a difference . . . even to God!

A Strong Impassibility Response

JAMES E. DOLEZAL

My disagreements with Thomas Jay Oord's chapter are several. I appreciate his acknowledgment of causality as a core issue in this debate but find his arguments for divine passibility to be either baseless or incoherent in import respects.

UNPROVEN ASSUMPTIONS ABOUT LOVE

Oord repeatedly insists that love necessarily entails give-and-take correlativity between the lover and the loved. This claim is indispensable to the integrity of his position, and yet I cannot see that he convincingly demonstrates the truth of it. How do we know that the Bible, though it freely depicts God's providential dealings with creatures in passibilist language, assumes God literally engages in a give-and-take relationship with creatures? We don't conclude that the Bible assumes divine materiality simply because it deploys corporealist language in relating God's providential dealings toward us. So why conclude it assumes the modality of passion in God simply because it deploys passibilist imagery to speak of him?

As for God's responses to human activity, impassibilists deny that these responses, insomuch as they are in God, are caused by the creature's action on him. Rather, God sovereignly ordains both human actions as well as his providential responses to them (see Is 46:9-11; Eph 1:11). We do not deny God responds to sin by offering forgiveness, but only deny that this merciful response is *caused* in him by his creatures. Oord's error seems to lie in his conflation of perfections, such as love and kindness, with the modality by which such perfections come to be in creatures. Creatures possess these perfections via an experience of passion (i.e., of receiving action on themselves); God possesses them as nothing but the superabundance of his purely actual being, and not as the effect of some agent's action on him.

IMITATION AND MODAL SAMENESS

A related problem emerges in Oord's assertion that the command for humans to imitate God's love and mercy means that God's love and mercy occur in a passible fashion. Oord presses for an inflexibly literal understanding of the term compassion, declaring it meaningless unless it includes all that belongs to empathetic suffering. Does Oord really believe language functions in such a suffocatingly precise manner? No one assumes that when we say we "grasp" an idea we have literally reached forth our hands and laid hold of it. We use the language analogously insomuch as the effect of grasping a thing with our hands and understanding a thing with our minds share the similar outcome of bringing a thing into our possession. So when Scripture speaks of God's compassion it need not be read as literally meaning that God cosuffers, but only that he acts on our behalf to do us good and give us comfort, like one who cosuffers with us in order to do us good.

Oord's argument also falters on the strange supposition that imitation requires modal sameness between the imitator and the imitated. Consider, for example, art's imitation of nature. The stars that appear in nature are luminous spheres of plasma with their own gravitational centers, whereas van Gogh's *The Starry Night* presents an image of such stars using oil on canvas. Van Gogh's circles of yellowish paint are genuine imitations, even if not exact modal reproductions of actual stars. When we see his painted stars, our thoughts are directed to the natural exemplars of which they are imitations; but we never think this means the night sky is really just a vast oil painting. We instinctively recognize that exemplars and their imitations need not exhibit modal sameness. Imitating God's love and mercy in accordance with our passible mode of being as humans does nothing to motivate the conclusion that God's love and mercy must exist in him via the same modalities of passion by which they exist in us.

OF NATURE AND EXPERIENCE

The most confusing set of claims in Oord's chapter appears in his discussion of nature and experience. "God's *nature*," he states, "is impassible and immutable.... God's essence is unchanging and unaffected by creation" (142). Yet Oord also contends that "engaging in giving-and-receiving relationships is an essential attribute of God" (145) and "being affected by others is a necessary attribute of God's nature" (145).

By affirming the immutability/impassibility of God's nature/essence, Oord could be saying one of two things: (1) that God's divinity, that form in virtue of which he is God, is unchangeable; or (2) that because of his immutable nature God is unable to be changed or moved. When impassibilists speak of the immutability/impassibility of God's nature, they primarily signify the latter (while not denying the former). Yet if Oord really agrees with them on this, then his argument that "God's actual *experience* is passible and mutable" would seem to indicate that God can have experiences that are wholly untethered from his nature. How God exists via his experiences is altogether incongruous with how he is by nature. Indeed, his nature would seem to indicate nothing about how he might be toward us in the purported give-and-take economy of creation and history.

Perhaps Oord only means to endorse option (1), in which case he says nothing unique about God. That's because creaturely natures/essences are also unchangeable (able to be exnihilated or annihilated, yes; but changed or mutated, no). Would Oord care to point to a concrete instance of creaturely nature/essence (note: not to a material subject or primary substance) in which some mutation has been undergone?

Impassibilists deny God has experiences insomuch as experience brings new knowledge of things to a subject based on a reality extrinsic to it. But God is not given new forms of knowledge or being by creatures (Is 40:13-14; cf. Rom 11:36). God has no experiences because he is purely actual and there is nothing the world has to give him that he lacks (Job 41:11). There is no creature that is that he does not make to be (Rev 4:11). There is nothing knowable in creation that does not proceed from his wisdom (Ps 104:24). And so there is no experience of creatures that could supply new forms of actuality to the divine being.

A Qualified Impassibility Response

DANIEL CASTELO

I happen to know Oord personally, and I find that this chapter exudes Oord's character in many ways. Rarely does one find a more charitable and likable interlocutor.

I find it very interesting that, like Dolezal, Oord assumes that the (im)passibility debates ultimately have to do with causality, with Oord taking the opposite stance to Dolezal, that humans influence or "relate" (his preferred term) to God as well as vice versa. Of course, Oord's view can account for a number of biblical patterns of speech, and as he notes early in his chapter, it also has the advantage of being appealing to the contemporary situation. Christology also plays a more central role in Oord's chapter than in Dolezal's.

For many today, Oord's proposals just make "more sense" than Dolezal's simply because they reflect better the conventions of thought characteristic of our moment. Whereas Dolezal's chapter runs the risk of deemphasizing the creaturely role in an effort to set-up and execute his preferred metaphysical apparatus, Oord's chapter runs the opposite risk, of potentially highlighting or elevating exceedingly the creaturely realm to the point that God (for some people's tastes at least) may sound too anthropomorphic. One could say that this risk is worth suffering, given the prominence of Dolezal's account within Western Christian antiquity. Personally, I do not think the matter should be cast as "pendulum swinging," although my presentation thus far may be heard as such.

One of the important contributions I see coming from Oord's chapter is the implication at work when he remarks, "And when we who are 'conformed to the image of his Son' express positive relations and appropriate emotions, we imitate the passible and emotional God (Rom 8:29)" (133). Operative here is the point that humans reflect God in that they are creatures created in the image of God. Could it be, given the witness of Scripture and the form of salvation history, that the image relates to affectivity somehow? On Dolezal's strict definitions and metaphysical parameters, the straightforward answer is no. Oord is willing to allow for this possibility, which I think is commendable because it allows for affectivity to be construed in positive ways, both in terms of the Creator and the creature. And this, I would say, is a very compelling move simply in terms of the incarnation itself: God in God's splendor has revealed Godself in terms of the human. Such an act muddies definitional exactitude, especially if it operates in terms of strict contrastives (such as that God is not a human and humans are not God). Both creation and incarnation push in the direction of connection and relatedness, and Oord attends to this. *I might question this*

Once one opens this door as Oord has, a follow-up question involves making the distinction between God and humans. Very well, if God and humans mutually influence one another, then what sets God apart? If God both gives and receives, as Oord finds it important to affirm, then the nature of God's reception has to be accounted for in a way that satisfies those who find that to be a threat to God's worship-worthiness because, as they hear it, such a claim makes God sound potentially deficient, fickle, and so "too human." I would say that the everyday believer would also be inclined to worry about a potentially unreliable or fickle God, all the while affirming God's relationality. What we are pressing toward is a both-and dynamic, something like a paradox or dialectic in which distinction and relationality are allowable. Oord hints at this when he opens the door to think of God as both perfectly unchanging and perfectly changing in different respects. He also makes this move when he draws the metaphysical distinction between God's essence being unchanging and God's experience being mutable.

A difficulty I see in Oord's presentation is a need for more substantiation related to the divine experience, and how this in turn must be accounted for, at least given our experience, in terms of history. As I mentioned above, we all have our metaphysical commitments, and this would be one feature that needs further clarification within Oord's proposals, especially if he wishes to be sympathetic to (if not altogether in agreement with) divine dipolarity. Also, I find the language of "necessity," given what Oord says immediately prior about the speculative nature of all theologizing, to be difficult to accommodate. The language exudes the kind of conceptual inflexibility that I am inclined to resist (and which, on occasion, Oord resists as well). But as I understand his view, the language of necessity fits well with what he says about theocosmocentrism. I am not inclined to think that Oord has characterized extensively enough some of the views that would compete with his preferred one, but it is clear here how Oord has opted for a metaphysical proposal that has God creating everlastingly, thereby questioning "creation from nothing" accounts. What I see with the language of necessity in Oord is a moral/character claim, especially in light of his three diagnostic questions (149). The challenge with Oord's presentation here is that necessity is coupled with control. I find control to be a corollary to the common element he shares with Dolezal, namely causality. Causality and control again function as a single coin, as one spectrum.

In my way of thinking, this suggests that the terms themselves, if they tend toward "both-and" affirmations, are ultimately inadequate. Reading both Dolezal and Oord together makes me wish to start the discussion over again with new terms, ones that do not rely fundamentally on some kind of logic of causality.

A Qualified Passibility Response

JOHN C. PECKHAM

There is much in Oord's essay with which I agree as well as some crucial areas in which we disagree. I agree that God is relational and passible and that creation makes a difference to God. Further, I greatly appreciate Oord's emphasis on how divine passibility holds significant practical implications relative to prayer, empathy (particularly with the oppressed), and exhortations to reflect God's love to others.

However, I fundamentally disagree with Oord's view regarding God's "essential relatedness" (129). In my view, God is not essentially related to the world but is *voluntarily* passible in relation to the world, meaning the omnipotent God, who needs nothing, freely chose to create this world and be affected by it in a way that maintains the Creator-creature distinction. I thus differ with Oord in significant ways regarding the nature of divine passibility and the nature of the God-world relationship.

One can agree with Oord that love is an essential divine attribute without holding that God is essentially related *to the world*. In my view, God is essentially related in love as Trinity (cf. Jn 17:24) and God's relational love for creatures is rooted in God's nature of love. Seeing the Trinity as "essentially relational" in love, however, does not require that God is essentially related to creation.

Contra Oord's "theocosmocentrism" (146), I maintain that God *freely* chose to create the world *ex nihilo* (see Ps 33:6; Heb 11:3; cf. Gen 1:1; Is 40:26-28; Neh 9:6) such that creation is neither eternal nor essentially related to God, by whom "all things . . . were created" and who is "before all things" (Col 1:16-17; cf. Ps 90:2; Jn 1:3; Rom 11:36). Given that Scripture maintains that God does not *need* anything (Acts 17:25), it follows that God does not *need anything* relative to his existence (aseity) to be who he is essentially (self-sufficiency). Accordingly, Revelation 4:11 praises God: "for you created all things, / and by your will they existed, and were created" (cf. Is 43:7). If it were not for God's freely bestowed grace and voluntary love (see Hos 14:4; Ex 33:19), creatures would not exist.

Whereas Oord's "essential kenosis" theology maintains that God could *not* have remained unchanged and unaffected by any world, in my view God *need not* have created or entered into any relationship with creatures but freely did so in a way that was congruent with his essential nature and character of love but not necessitated by it (in strong contrast to process and other such conceptions). Further, contra Oord, I believe that God does possess exhaustive definite foreknowledge. Whereas I do think instances of divine *nāḥam* provide evidence of divine passibility (e.g., Gen 6:6; Jer 18:7-10), I do not believe such instances indicate that "God changes plans" in the sense that God did not foreknow what would occur.

Finally, I turn to Oord's claims that the view that God is not essentially related to the world in love: (1) makes God's love arbitrary, (2) negates grounds for assurance of God's continued love, and (3) lacks "grounds for believing it is *necessarily* true that God will never 'leave you or forsake you'" (149).

Regarding the first claim, if God's relational love for creation is rooted in God's essential nature of love, as I maintain, it does not follow that contingent aspects of God's love in relation to creatures would be merely arbitrary, much less God's love on the whole. For example, I did not *need* to have a son. My wife and I chose to try to have a child. Yet it would be deeply mistaken to characterize my love for my son as arbitrary as if I could just as easily love Ebenezer Scrooge as I do my own son.

Further, I do not see on what basis one can persuasively claim that God would have been "selfish" had he not created the world (146); as if creatures are entitled to being created. Would it not be strange indeed for me to charge my wife—who does love me greatly and undeservedly—with selfishness because she *might* not have loved me? Similarly, it seems misguided to criticize God for being able to not have done what he has done!

Consider the cross event. "No one" takes Christ's life; Christ states, "I lay it down of my own accord" (Jn 10:18), demonstrating God's unselfish love for us (Rom 5:8). In my view, any worry that God might be selfish is more than dealt with by the fact that Christ voluntarily condescended to lay down his life for us (Phil 2:5-11; Jn 15:13).

Further, contra Oord, without positing any essential relation between God and creation, we can have assurance that God's *disposition* of love does not change because God never lies (Titus 1:2) and himself declares, "I have loved you with an everlasting love" (Jer 31:3). In this regard, Scripture affirms that while God's disposition of love (God's essential nature) is everlasting, and always unmerited, it is also (relationally) contingent *in some respects* (Ps 103:17; cf. Jer 16:5; Hos 9:15).[1]

Yet, if we believe God's promises, grounded in the "unchangeableness of His purpose," regarding "which it is impossible for God to lie" (Heb 6:17-18 NASB), then we need not maintain that God is essentially relational in order to be confident that God will do as he says and "never leave" or "forsake" his people (Heb 13:5; Deut 31:6). In my view, the covenantal, promise-keeping God of the cross provides more than sufficient assurance of the steadfastness of God's love.

In this regard, I believe qualified passibility is preferable to strong passibility because it can consistently affirm the biblical testimony regarding God's passible emotions and love relationship with the world, while also maintaining what I believe Scripture affirms—*both* divine freedom in relation to the world *and* that God is not dependent on anything else relative to his existence (aseity) or essential nature (self-sufficiency).

---

[1]See John C. Peckham, *The Love of God: A Canonical Model* (Downers Grove, IL: IVP Academic, 2015), 199-214.

Concluding Remarks in Defense of Strong Passibility

THOMAS JAY OORD

I'm grateful to this book's editors and my dialogue partners. Not only have we described our views on God's passibility (or lack thereof), we've pushed the conversation in deeper and novel ways. I appreciate that my dialogue partners pushed me to articulate my views more clearly.

I begin this final set of observations with James E. Dolezal's response to my essay. I take it as self-evident that love is relational. Dolezal does not. I take the biblical language about God being affected by others as straightforwardly true. Dolezal does not. I believe thinking God's love is relational—in the sense of giving and receiving—makes excellent sense of the Bible and everyday life. Dolezal opts for a nonrelational God. I think imitating God's love requires that both God and creatures are in some senses relational. Dolezal doesn't. I think God's nature is unchanging and impassible, while God's experience changes and is passible. Dolezal seems not to fathom this approach.

I'm not surprised Dolezal does not endorse my proposals on passibility. After all, his views and mine are more unlike than any in this book. I suspect that we have different metaphysical intuitions. I don't find his intuitions satisfying; he doesn't find mine satisfying. It's no wonder we see God's relationality very differently.

Daniel Castelo and I have, by contrast, much in common. He sees the value of my position when it comes to imitating Christ. Castelo rightly sees that imitating Christ amounts to more than just external actions; we can also imitate Christ in our emotions. Castelo also sees that my view overcomes the worry that a relational/passible God might be fickle or too much like humans. In my view, the Creator is not like creatures, because God's nature is immutable and impassible. I affirm God's ethical immutability.

Castelo does have a few worries with my view. He worries about my claims of divine "necessities." Perhaps this worry would also disappear were he to see that I don't think of necessity as a form of what he calls "conceptual inflexibility" (157). The necessities to which I refer derive from the immutability of God's nature not any inflexibilities in my scheme.

Castelo is not yet ready to affirm theocosmocentrism nor yet ready to reject creation from nothing. I'm not surprised by this because such moves required further reflection. I'm not sure what he means by saying I couple necessity with control, so I'll look forward to discussing this and other issues more in future interactions.

Castelo concludes his reflections on my work by wishing we could start the impassibility conversation over with terms that don't require causality. By contrast, I think the language of causality is essential to this discussion. But by "causality," I don't mean God acts as a sufficient cause. I simply mean God affects us and we affect God, which implies some measure of causality.

John C. Peckham and I agree on so much. But his response highlights our disagreements. Much of his response rehashes his article's view that God's relationship with the world is entirely voluntary and not essential. In other words, he doesn't think God necessarily loves us. I do.

I already addressed the problems with Peckham's views of impassibility in my response to his essay (120-24), and I encourage readers to look at that response again in light of his response to my essay. In my response, I affirmed that strong passibility could mean God essentially relates in Trinity. But I showed the problems with thinking God only relates essentially among three persons in the Trinity but is not essentially related to creation. Believing God created the universe *ex nihilo* implies that God relates arbitrarily to us.

One issue I did not address in my original criticism seems important here. That issue is Peckham's appeal to biblical passages. He and I agree that we both view the Bible highly. We both take the Bible as our primary source for theological work. We both claim to be biblical theologians in the broad sense of the term.

What troubles me about Peckham's writings in general and his response to my essay, in particular, is the way he often appeals to biblical passages. These appeals often do not explicitly support his views nor explicitly deny mine. For instance, in his response he says, "contra Oord's 'theocosmocentrism,' I maintain that God *freely* chose to create the world *ex nihilo* (see Ps 33:6; Heb 11:3; cf. Gen 1:1; Is 40:26-28; Neh 9:6) such that creation is neither eternal nor essentially related to God, by whom 'all things . . . were created' and who is 'before all things' (Col 1:16-17; cf. Ps 90:2; Jn 1:3; Rom 11:36)" (158-59). Notice all the biblical references sprinkled in the sentence, giving the impression to the reader that the Bible supports Peckham's views and not mine.

If we look at all the biblical passages Peckham splashes in this section and others, we find that *none* explicitly endorse his views over mine. None. But his use of them gives the impression that the Bible explicitly supports his view over mine. I find this mistake often in Peckham's response and essay. The casual reader may be impressed when he adds such references, thinking Peckham's views have biblical support and mine do not. But this reader would have been misled.

To be specific, I know of no biblical passage that explicitly tells us whether God essentially or contingently relates to creation. It's legitimate to make inferences about God's relation with creation, of course. I do that and so do others. But Peckham seems to be trying to signal to his readers that the Bible is decidedly on his side on the question of God's essential relations. But it is not. Or take the *creatio ex nihilo* references Peckham pastes after he says, "God *freely* chose to create the world *ex nihilo*." None explicitly support his view. Adding these references wrongly gives the naïve reader the idea that the Bible explicitly supports Peckham's view that God freely created the world from nothingness. The Bible does not explicitly endorse that view.

I have no problem appealing to the Bible to support one's view. I do so often. But it's not helpful to paste biblical references to statements that don't explicitly support one's view, especially when doing so seems to signal to readers that the Bible supports one's own view and an opponent's view.

In the major part of Peckham's response to me, he addresses my criticism that his view affirms that God (1) loves creation arbitrarily, (2) cannot assure us of God's continued love, and (3) will never leave us nor forsake us.

In what follows, I'll argue that Peckham's responses to these three criticisms are mistaken.

On my claim that Peckham's view paints God's love for creatures as arbitrary, Peckham says, "I did not *need* to have a son. My wife and I chose to try to have a child. Yet, it would be deeply mistaken to characterize my love for my son as arbitrary as if I could just as easily love Ebenezer Scrooge as I do my own son" (159). But Peckham's love for his son *is* arbitrary! (And so is his love for Scrooge, for that matter.) He doesn't *have* to love his son. In fact, many human fathers do not love their sons. And assuming Peckham is not a perfect father, Peckham has occasionally acted in unloving ways toward his son. Peckham's love for his son is arbitrary, in the sense of contingent, because "love for others" is not an essential attribute in Peckham's nature. By contrast, I claim that love for creation is an essential aspect of God's nature. God *must* love creation because loving creaturely others is part of what it means to be divine. Peckham's love for his son is not necessary, so it's arbitrary/contingent. God's love for creation is necessary, so it's essential.

Peckham doesn't agree with my claim that a God who only loves in Trinity would be essentially self-centered and contingently altruistic. He can't understand how one would claim, "God would have been 'selfish' had he not created the world; as if creatures are entitled to being created. Would it not be strange indeed for me to charge my wife—who does love me greatly and undeservedly—with selfishness because she *might* not have loved me?" (159). Peckham misunderstands the argument I'm making. I claimed that a God who only necessarily loves in the Trinity does not express love necessarily for creation. Peckham's reference to his wife's love as an example fails. Neither Peckham nor I would say his wife necessarily loves him. I'm confident Peckham's wife chooses to love him, but her nature does not include "love for John" as a necessary and eternal attribute.

Peckham then tries to distinguish between God's disposition to love and God's relational love for us. "Without positing any essential relation between God and creation," he says, "we can have assurance that God's *disposition* of love does not change because God never lies (Titus 1:2) and himself declares, 'I have loved you with an everlasting love' (Jer 31:3)" (160). Notice the difference Peckham wants to make between love as a disposition and love as a relation. I claim they make far better sense when together. After all, it would be strange to say God has an essential disposition that God may choose *never* to express. It's like saying, "God's very heart is love for others, but God may never express love for others!" To put it technically, it makes little sense to say, "God's essence is other-oriented love, but God could have chosen never to love others."

Instead of saying love for others is God's very essence, Peckham thinks we can trust the God who arbitrarily loves creation never to leave us nor forsake us. He appeals to the cross of Christ to support this view. I join Peckham in thinking the cross points to God's love for us. But because I believe God necessarily loves creation, I am assured of this in a way Peckham cannot be!

I conclude this essay with sentiments I expressed at the outset. I'm grateful! Dolezal, Castelo, and Peckham have pushed me to think in new and deeper ways. The dialogue has brought new insights. I thank them and the editors for inviting me to this exploration of God's passibility.

Conclusion

ROBERT J. MATZ AND A. CHADWICK THORNHILL

So is God impassible and unaffected by his creation, necessarily uncontrolling and influenced by his creatures, or somewhere in between? We leave it to the reader to decide which essay was a most convincing interpretation of the biblical and theological data which surround the question of God's (im)passibility. A few observations may be helpful to serve the reader as they reflect on the contents of the volume.

First, as has been displayed throughout, different methodological and presuppositional factors contribute to the positions each author has developed. In the first essay, Dolezal maintains that impassibility is a necessity to safeguard the doctrine of God from error. In speaking of actuality to frame the debate, Dolezal suggests that God is either being or becoming, meaning that on an impassibilist account, God's nature is unchanging, and on a passibilist account, it is not. For Dolezal, without the doctrine of impassibility, and its related doctrines, God cannot be spoken of as unchanging in any regard. God receiving or being affected by his creatures indicates some deficiency in God. In conjunction with divine aseity, pure actuality, and divine simplicity, impassibility produces a "dynamic stillness" by which God's emotions are unchanging and unaffected, and thereby constant. Dolezal's case is made by considering biblical texts in conversation with the "historical grammar" he unpacks, largely from his interactions with Aquinas. He finds emotional descriptions of God in Scripture as "anthropopathic," meaning described in human terms but only because of the limitations of humans, not because they are adequate descriptions for God.

Daniel Castelo seeks a mediating place between strong impassibility and strong passibility. Castelo offers a narrative of sorts tracing the development of his own thoughts on impassibility, which largely began through interaction with Moltmann. He also examines some Western cultural trajectories that he finds have influenced our thoughts on God, particularly as related to God's nature. Castelo recognizes that the complicated conversations throughout Christian history must be both appropriated but also appreciated in their own contextual setting. This means that all of our language and talk about God is conditioned, inadequate, and incomplete. He finds binary thinking about (im)passibility unhelpful and suggests that an apophatic context for impassibility can shed light on how we absorb the doctrine. Impassibility can help to reinforce the Creator-creature distinction while also reinforcing the paradoxical nature of Christian belief.

John C. Peckham offers a qualified version of passibility. Peckham offers a canonical case for qualified passibility, which he frames as a voluntary passibility that God freely chose, opening himself to being affected by the world while not negating the Creator-creature distinction. He offers his case by working to develop a "biblical congruency" on the issue. He notes numerous instances where in Scripture God is affected by or responds to his human creatures on a relational or emotional level. While he agrees that there are imperfect analogies at work between divine and human emotions, he finds the weight of the biblical data sufficient to ground belief in a voluntarily passible God. God is voluntarily affected, so Peckham argues his nature is not challenged or changed because God wills and allows this to be so.

Finally, Thomas Jay Oord offers a strong view of passibility. Oord argues that God is essentially related to creation, meaning his openness to the world and to being affected by his creatures is an essential aspect of who God is. Oord finds the extensiveness of the biblical data about God's relational nature and emotions compelling, along with the incarnation, which displays a passible God in a passible Jesus. Oord finds God the "most moved mover," meaning he is affected and thereby changed by his interactions with his creatures. For Oord, the practical payoff of such a view of God underscores the reality of prayer, God as empathetic, and God as able to be imitated. Were passibility not a reality of God, for Oord these dimensions of divine-human interactions would not exist.

As the reader may have also observed, the way in which different theological voices are called to aid in the theological task is not uniform. We mentioned in the introduction that the patristic writers are often called to both sides of the debate in this issue, as they are with a host of other theological issues. Throughout this volume, Reformation, post-Reformation, and modern voices have been called on in support of opposing theological perspectives. This reminds us all the more of the care and compassion that is needed when interacting with these other voices and seeing them first as conversation partners in their own right from within their theological contexts. It also demonstrates the value we hope this publication will bring to the conversation in clarifying the spectrum of current positions and establishing the need to better define terms and concepts in the debate.

To return to the questions which have framed these responses, we ask the reader to return afresh and consider for themselves what biblical, theological, and philosophical articulations may emerge having interacted with this volume: (1) Is God's emotional life analogous to the human emotional life? (2) Are God's nature, will, and knowledge passible, and to what extent? (3) Does human activity (such as prayer) occasion an emotive/volitional response from God? (4) Do the incarnation and passion of Jesus Christ necessitate passibility?

Finally, we believe it is also helpful to reflect not only on the contents of this volume as it relates to the question of (im)passibility, but also on some of the virtues portrayed within. The task of theology is not one that should be entered into lightly. As the contributors of this volume have demonstrated, a careful and patient interaction with the biblical text, Christian tradition, philosophy, and one's own cultural context is necessary in the task. Furthermore, just as language must be disciplined, so must the theologian, both in the care with which they undertake their work and in their pursuit of Christ as a disciple. The Christian nature of theology, in the sense of pursuing theology as followers of Christ, means humility, fairness, and conviction should be exercised in the theological task. We pray this book has been a means to affect such ends of clarity and charity in Christian theology.

Bibliography

Anselm. *Basic Writings*, translated by Thomas Williams. Indianapolis: Hackett, 2007.

Aquinas, Thomas. *Summa Theologiae: Complete English Edition in Five Volumes*. Translated by the Fathers of the English Dominican Province. 5 vols. Westminster, MD: Christian Classics, 1981.

Arminius, Jacobus. *The Works of James Arminius*, translated by James Nichols, William Nichols, and Carl Bangs. 3 vols. Grand Rapids: Baker, 1986.

Baines, Ron, ed. *Confessing the Impassible God: The Biblical, Classical, and Confessional Doctrine of Divine Impassibility*. Palmdale, CA: Reformed Baptist Academic Press, 2015.

Baker, Chris, et al., eds. *Uncontrolling Love: Essays Exploring the Love of God, with Introductory Essays by Thomas Jay Oord*. San Diego, CA: SacraSage, 2017.

Barth, Karl. *Church Dogmatics*, translated by G. W. Bromiley and Thomas F. Torrance. 14 vols. Peabody, MA: Hendrickson Publishers, 2010.

Bauckham, Richard. "In Defence of *The Crucified God*." In *The Power and Weakness of God: Impassibility and Orthodoxy*, edited by Nigel M. de S. Cameron. Edinburgh: Rutherford House, 1990.

———. *Jesus and the God of Israel: God Crucified and Other Studies on the New Testament's Christology of Divine Identity*. Grand Rapids: Eerdmans, 2008.

Bavinck, Herman. *Reformed Dogmatics*, edited by John Bolt. Translated by John Vried. 4 vols. Grand Rapids: Baker, 2008.

Bonhoeffer, Dietrich. *Letters and Papers from Prison*. Dietrich Bonhoeffer Works, vol. 8. Minneapolis: Fortress, 2009.

———. *The Cost of Discipleship*. New York: Macmillan, 1949.

Boyd, Gregory A. *Is God to Blame? Beyond Pat Answers to the Problem of Suffering*. Downers Grove, IL: InterVarsity Press, 2003.

Brenner, Athalya, ed. *The Feminist Companion to the Bible*, vol. 8: *A Feminist Companion to the Latter Prophets*. Sheffield: Sheffield Academic Press, 1995.

Brueggemann, Walter. "The Recovering God of Hosea." *Horizons in Biblical Theology* 30 (2008): 5-20.

———. *Theology of the Old Testament: Testimony, Dispute, Advocacy*. Minneapolis: Fortress, 1997.

Calvin, John. *Commentaries on the First Book of Moses Called Genesis*, translated by John King. 2 vols. Grand Rapids: Eerdmans, 1948.

———. *Commentaries on the Twelve Minor Prophets*. Translated by John Owen. Grand Rapids: Eerdmans, 1950.

Carson, D. A. *The Difficult Doctrine of the Love of God*. Wheaton, IL: Crossway, 2000.

Castelo, Daniel. "Moltmann's Dismissal of Divine Impassibility: Warranted?" *Scottish Journal of Theology* 61 (2008): 396-407.

———. "Only the Impassible God Can Help: Moltmann and the Contemporary Status of Divine Impassibility." PhD diss., Duke University, 2005.

———. *The Apathetic God: Exploring the Contemporary Relevance of Divine Impassibility*. Paternoster Theological Monographs. Eugene, OR: Wipf and Stock Publishers, 2009.

Chan, Michael J. and Brent A. Strawn, ed. *What Kind of God? Collected Essays of Terence E. Fretheim*. Winona Lake, IN: Eisenbrauns, 2015.

Charnock, Stephen and William Symington. *The Existence and Attributes of God*. 2 vols. 1853. Reprint, Grand Rapids: Baker, 1979.

Clayton, Philip and Arthur Peacocke, eds. *In Whom We Live and Move and Have Our Being: Panentheistic Reflections on God's Presence in a Scientific World*. Grand Rapids: Eerdmans, 2004.

Cobb Jr., John B. *God and the World*. Philadelphia: Westminster, 1969.

Cone, James. *God of the Oppressed*, rev. ed. Maryknoll, NY: Orbis, 1997.

Creel, Richard. *Divine Impassibility: An Essay in Philosophical Theology*. New York: Cambridge University Press, 1986.

Cross, Frank L. and E. A. Livingstone, eds. *The Oxford Dictionary of the Christian Church*, 3rd ed. New York: Oxford University Press, 2005.

Culpepper, Gary. "'One Suffering, in Two Natures': An Analogical Inquiry into Divine and Human Suffering." In *Divine Impassibility and the Mystery of Human Suffering*, edited by James Keating and Thomas Joseph White. Grand Rapids: Eerdmans, 2009.

Cyril. *Cyril of Alexandria, Select Letters*, translated by Lionel R. Wickham. Oxford Early Christian Texts. Oxford: Clarendon Press, 1983.

————. *St. Cyril of Alexandria* in Vladimir's Seminary Press Popular Patristics Series. Vol. 13, *On the Unity of Christ*, translated by John Anthony McGuckin. Crestwood, NY: St. Vladimir's Seminary Press, 1995.

Danker, Frederick W., et al., eds. *A Greek-English Lexicon of the New Testament and Other Early Christian Literature*. 3rd ed. Chicago: University of Chicago Press, 2000.

Dawkins, Richard. *The God Delusion*. Boston: Houghton Mifflin, 2006.

Dodds, Michael J. *The Unchanging God of Love: Thomas Aquinas and Contemporary Theology on Divine Immutability*. 2nd ed. Washington, DC: Catholic University of America Press, 2008.

Dolezal, James E. *All That Is in God: Evangelical Theology and the Challenge of Classical Christian Theism*. Grand Rapids: Reformation Heritage Books, 2017.

————. *God Without Parts: Divine Simplicity and the Metaphysics of God's Absoluteness*. Eugene, OR: Pickwick, 2011.

————. "Still Impassible: Confessing God Without Passions." *Journal of the Institute of Reformed Baptist Studies* 1 (2014): 125-51.

Dorner, Isaak August. "The History of the Doctrine of the Immutability of God." In *Divine Immutability*, translated by Robert R. Williams and Claude Welch. Minneapolis: Fortress, 1994.

Duby, Steven J. *Divine Simplicity: A Dogmatic Account*. T&T Clark Studies in Systematic Theology. New York: T&T Clark, 2018.

Dunning, H. Ray. *Grace, Faith, and Holiness*. Kansas City, MO: Beacon Hill, 1988.

Emery, Giles, O. P. "The Immutability of the God of Love and the Problem of Language Concerning the 'Suffering of God.'" In *Divine Impassibility and the Mystery of Human Suffering*, edited by James F. Keating and Thomas Joseph White. Grand Rapids: Eerdmans, 2009.

Feinberg, John S. *No One Like Him: The Doctrine of God*. Wheaton, IL: Crossway, 2001.

Feser, Edward. *Scholastic Metaphysics: A Contemporary Introduction*. Neunkirchen-Seelscheid: Editiones Scholasticae, 2014.

Fiddes, Paul. *The Creative Suffering of God*. New York: Oxford University Press, 1988.

Fretheim, Terence E. *God and World in the Old Testament: A Relational Theology of Creation*. Nashville: Abingdon Press, 2005.

————. *The Suffering of God: An Old Testament Perspective*. Overtures to Biblical Theology. Minneapolis, Fortress Press, 1984.

————. "The Repentance of God: A Key to Evaluating Old Testament God-Talk." *Horizons in Biblical Theology* 10, no. 1 (1988): 47-80.

Fritsch, Charles T. *The Anti-Anthropomorphisms of the Greek Pentateuch*. Princeton: Princeton University Press, 1943.

Gavrilyuk, Paul L. *The Suffering of the Impassible God: The Dialectics of Patristic Thought*. The Oxford Early Christian Studies. New York: Oxford University Press, 2004.

———. "God's Impassible Suffering in the Flesh: The Promise of Paradoxical Christology." In *Divine Impassibility and the Mystery of Human Suffering*, edited by James F. Keating and Thomas Joseph White. Grand Rapids: Eerdmans, 2009.

Gill, John. *Gill's Commentaries*. 6 vols. Grand Rapids: Baker Books House, 1980.

Goldingay, John. *Daniel*. Word Biblical Commentary. Dallas: Word, 1989.

Goldingay, John. *Old Testament Theology*, vol. 1: *Israel's Gospel*. Downers Grove, IL: InterVarsity Press, 1993.

Gondreau, Paul. *The Passions of Christ's Soul in the Theology of St. Thomas Aquinas*. Münster: Aschendorff Verlag, 2002.

Gorman, Michael. *Aquinas on the Metaphysics of the Hypostatic Union*. New York: Cambridge University Press, 2017.

Griffin, Jeffery D. "An Investigation of Idiomatic Expressions in the Hebrew Bible with a Case Study of Anatomical Idioms." PhD diss., Mid-America Baptist Theological Seminary, 1999.

Grudem, Wayne. *Systematic Theology*. Grand Rapids: Zondervan, 1994.

Harnack, Adolf von. *What Is Christianity?* Fortress Texts in Modern Theology. Translated by T. Bailey Saunders and Rudolf Bultmann. Philadelphia: Fortress, 1986.

Hart, David Bentley. "No Shadow of Turning: On Divine Impassibility." *Pro Ecclesia* 11, no. 2 (2002): 184-206.

Hartshorne, Charles. *Man's Vision of God and the Logic of Theism*. Chicago and New York: Willett, Clark, and Co., 1941.

———. *The Divine Relativity*. New Haven, CT: Yale University Press, 1948.

Held, Shai. *Abraham Joshua Heschel: The Call of Transcendence*. Bloomington: Indiana University Press, 2013.

Helm, Paul. "B. B. Warfield on Divine Passion." *Westminster Theological Journal* 69, no. 1 (2007): 94-104.

———. "The Impossibility of Divine Passibility." In *The Power and Weakness of God: Impassibility and Orthodoxy*, edited by Nigel M. de S. Cameron. Edinburgh: Rutherford House, 1990.

Henry, Carl F. H. *God, Revelation, and Authority: The God Who Stands and Stays, Part One*, vol. 5. Waco: Word, 1982.

Henry, Matthew A. *Matthew Henry's Commentary on the Whole Bible: In Six Volumes Carefully Revised and Corrected*. 6 Vols. London: Fleming H. Revell, 1983.

Heschel, Abraham. *The Prophets*. New York: Harper and Row, 1962.

Hillers, Delbert R. *Treaty-Curses and the Old Testament Prophets*. Rome: Pontifical Biblical Institute, 1964.

Jenni, Ernst and Claus Westermann, ed. *Theological Lexicon of the Old Testament*. Peabody, MA: Hendrickson Publishers, 1990.

Kelle, Brad E. "Hosea 1–3 in Twentieth Century Scholarship." *Currents in Biblical Research* 7 (2009): 177-218.

Keller, Catherine. *From a Broken Web: Separation, Sexism and Self*. Boston: Beacon Press, 1986.

Kennedy, Geoffrey Anketell Studdert. *The Hardest Part*. London: Hodder and Stoughton, 1918.

Kitamori, Kazoh. *Theology of the Pain of God*, 5th ed. Richmond, VA: John Knox Press, 1965.

Kittel, Gerhard and G. W. Bromiley. *Theological Dictionary of the New Testament*. 10 vols. Grand Rapids: Eerdmans, 1964-1976.

Klubertanz, George Peter. *Introduction to the Philosophy of Being*. 2nd ed. Eugene, OR: Wipf & Stock, 2005.

Koehler, Ludwig and Walter Baumgartner. *Hebrew and Aramaic Lexicon on the Old Testament*. Leiden: Brill, 1996.

Lee, Jung Young. *God Suffers for Us*. Netherlands: Martinus Nijhoff, The Hague, 1974.

Lim, Bo H. and Daniel Castelo. *Hosea*. Two Horizons Old Testament Commentary. Grand Rapids: Eerdmans, 2015.

Lister, Rob. *God Is Impassible and Impassioned: Toward a Theology of Divine Emotion*. Wheaton, IL: Crossway, 2013.

McCormack, Bruce. "Divine Impassibility or Simply Divine Constancy: Implications for Karl Barth's Later Christology for Debates over Impassibility." In *Divine Impassibility and the Mystery of Human Suffering*, edited by James F. Keating and Thomas Joseph White. Grand Rapids: Eerdmans, 2009.

McGuckin, John. *Saint Cyril of Alexandria and the Christological Controversy*. Crestwood: St. Vladimir's Seminary Press, 2004.

Miner, Robert C. *Thomas Aquinas on the Passions: A Study of* Summa Theologiae. New York: Cambridge University Press, 2009.

Moberly, R. W. L. *Old Testament Theology: Reading the Hebrew Bible as Christian Scripture*. Grand Rapids: Baker Academic, 2013.

Moltmann, Jürgen. *The Crucified God: The Cross of Christ as the Foundation and Criticism of Christian Theology*. Minneapolis: Fortress, 1993.

———. *The Trinity and the Kingdom: The Doctrine of God*. Minneapolis: Fortress, 1993.

Mullins, R. T. *The End of the Timeless God*. Oxford Studies in Analytic Theology. New York: Oxford University Press, 2015.

———. "Impassibility, Omnisubjectivity, and the Problem of Unity in Love." In *Love, Human and Divine: Contemporary Essays in Systematic and Philosophical Theology*, edited by Oliver D. Crisp, James Arcadi, and Jordan Wessling. New York: Bloomsbury, 2019.

Nicholson, Ernest W. *God and His People*. Oxford: Clarendon, 1986.

Oord, Thomas J. *Defining Love: A Philosophical, Scientific, and Theological Engagement*. Grand Rapids: Brazos, 2010.

———, ed. *Theologies of Creation: Ex Nihilo and its New Rivals*. New York: Routledge, 2014.

———. *The Nature of Love: A Theology*. St. Louis: Chalice, 2010.

———. *The Uncontrolling Love of God: An Open and Relational Account of Providence*. Downers Grove, IL: IVP Academic, 2015.

Oswalt, John N. *Isaiah 40–66*. New International Commentary on the Old Testament. Grand Rapids: Eerdmans, 1998.

Parunak, H. Van Dyke. "A Semantic Survey of *Nhm*." *Biblica* 56 (1975): 512-32.

Peckham, John C. *The Concept of Divine Love in the Context of the God-World Relationship*. Studies in Biblical Literature. New York: Peter Lang, 2014.

———. *The Love of God: A Canonical Model*. Downers Grove, IL: IVP Academic, 2015.

———. *Canonical Theology: The Biblical Canon, Sola Scriptura, and Theological Method*. Grand Rapids: Eerdmans, 2016.

Pinnock, Clark et. al., *The Openness of God: A Biblical Challenge to the Traditional Understand of God*. Downers Grove, IL: InterVarsity Press, 1994.

———. *Most Moved Mover: A Theology of God's Openness*. Grand Rapids: Baker Academic, 2001.

Placher, William. *Narratives of a Vulnerable God: Christ, Theology, and Scripture*. Louisville: Westminster John Knox, 1994.

Pomplun, Trent. "Impassibility in St. Hilary of Poitiers's *De Trinitate*." In *Divine Impassibility and the Mystery of Human Suffering*, edited by James F. Keating and Thomas Joseph White. Grand Rapids: Eerdmans, 2009.

Pool, Jeff. *God's Wounds: Hermeneutic of the Christian Symbol of Divine Suffering*, vol. 1: *Divine Vulnerability and Creation*. Cambridge: James Clarke and Co., 2009.

Renihan, Samuel. *God Without Passions: A Reader*. Palmdale, CA: Reformed Baptist Academic Press, 2015.

Roberts, Alexander, and James Donaldson, eds. *Ante-Nicene Fathers*. 10 vols. Buffalo, NY: The Christian Literature Company, 1885–1887.

Roberts, Alexander, and James Donaldson, eds. *Nicene and Post-Nicene Fathers*. 14 vols. Buffalo, NY: The Christian Literature Company, 1885–1887.

Rocca, Gregory P. *Speaking the Incomprehensible God: Thomas Aquinas on the Interplay of Positive and Negative Theology*. Washington, DC: Catholic University of America Press, 2008.

Rutledge, Fleming. *The Crucifixion: Understanding the Death of Christ*. Grand Rapids: Eerdmans, 2015.

Sanders, John. "Historical Considerations." In *The Openness of God: A Biblical Challenge to the Traditional Understanding of God*. Downers Grove, IL: InterVarsity Press, 1994.

———. *The God Who Risks: A Theology of Divine Providence*. Downers Grove, IL: IVP Academic, 2007.

Sarot, Marcel. *God, Possibility, and Corporeality*. Leuven: Peeters, 1992.

Shah, Farhan A. "Toward a Process-Humanistic Interpretation of Islam: An Examination of Muhammed Iqbal's God Concept." Master's Thesis, University of Oslo, 2016.

Sirvent, Robert. *Embracing Vulnerability: Human and Divine*. Eugene, OR: Pickwick, 2014.

Smith, J. Warren. "Suffering Impassibly: Christ's Passion in Cyril of Alexandria's Soteriology." *Pro Ecclesia* 11 (2002): 463-83.

Stott, John. *The Cross of Christ*. Downers Grove, IL: InterVarsity Press, 2006.

Taliaferro, Charles. "The Passibility of God." *Religious Studies* 25, no. 2 (1989): 217-24.

———. *Consciousness and the Mind of God*. New York: Cambridge University Press, 1994.

Thompson, J. A. *Jeremiah*. New International Commentary on the Old Testament. Grand Rapids: Eerdmans, 1980.

Torrance, Alan. "Does God Suffer? Incarnation and Impassibility." In *Christ in Our Place: The Humanity of God in Christ for the Reconciliation of the World*, edited by Trevor A. Hart. Eugene, OR: Wipf and Stock, 1989.

Torrance, T. F. *The Christian Doctrine of God*. New York: Continuum, 1996.

United Methodist Hymnal: Book of United Methodist Worship. Nashville: United Methodist Publishing House, 1989.

VanGemeren, Willem A. *New International Dictionary of Old Testament Theology and Exegesis*. 5 vols. Grand Rapids: Zondervan, 2012.

Vanhoozer, Kevin J. *First Theology: God, Scripture, and Hermeneutics*. Downers Grove, IL: IVP Academic, 2002.

————. "Love Without Measure? John Webster's Unfinished Dogmatic Account of the Love of God, in Dialogue with Thomas Jay Oord's Interdisciplinary Theological Account." *International Journal of Systematic Theology* 19, no. 4 (Oct 2017): 505-26.

————. *Remythologizing Theology*. New York: Cambridge University Press, 2010.

Ware, Bruce A. "An Evangelical Reexamination of the Doctrine of the Immutability of God." PhD Dissertation, Fuller Theological Seminary, 1984.

Weigel, Peter J. *Aquinas on Simplicity: An Investigation into the Foundations of His Philosophical Theology*. Oxford: Peter Lang, 2008.

Weinandy, Thomas G. *Does God Suffer?* Notre Dame, IN: University of Notre Dame, 2000.

————. *Studies in Historical Theology*, vol. 4: *Does God Change? The Word's Becoming in the Incarnation*. Still River, MA: St. Bede's Publications, 1985.

Wesley, John. *Explanatory Notes upon the Old Testament*. 3 Vols. Bristol: William Pine, 1765.

Whitehead, Alfred North. *Process and Reality: An Essay in Cosmology*, corrected edition by David Ray Griffin and Donald W. Sherburne. New York: Free Press, 1978.

Williams, Daniel Day. "Suffering and Being in Empirical Theology." In *The Future of Empirical Theology*, edited by B. L. Meland. Chicago: University of Chicago Press, 1969.

Willis, John T. "The 'Repentance' of God in the Books of Samuel, Jeremiah, and Jonah." *Horizons in Biblical Theology* 16 (1994): 156-76.

Wippel, John F. *The Metaphysical Thought of Thomas Aquinas: From Finite Being to Uncreated Being*. Washington: Catholic University of America Press, 2000.

Wolterstorff, Nicholas. "Suffering Love." In *Philosophy and the Christian Faith*, edited by Thomas V. Morris. Notre Dame, IN: University of Notre Dame Press, 1990.

Wuellner, Bernard J. *Dictionary of Scholastic Philosophy*. Fitzwilliam, New Hampshire: Loreto Publications, 2012.

Contributors

Daniel Castelo (PhD, Duke University) is professor of dogmatic and constructive theology at Seattle Pacific University. He is the author of numerous books, including *The Apathetic God: Exploring the Contemporary Relevance of Divine Impassibility*, *Theological Theodicy*, and *Pentecostalism as a Christian Mystical Tradition*. In addition to his work on theology proper, Castelo is an ordained elder in the Pacific Northwest Conference of the Free Methodist Church.

James E. Dolezal (PhD, Westminster Theological Seminary) is assistant professor of theology in the School of Divinity at Cairn University. Prior to his current appointment, he served as the pastor of a Reformed Baptist church in Alberta, Canada. He is the author of *God Without Parts: Divine Simplicity and the Metaphysics of God's Absoluteness* and *All That Is in God: Evangelical Theology and the Challenge of Classical Christian Theism*.

Robert J. Matz (PhD, Liberty University) is assistant professor of Christian studies at Midwestern Baptist Theological Seminary. He has contributed to several books and has two additional forthcoming volumes. In addition to his responsibilities at Midwestern, he pastors a Baptist church in the Kansas City area.

Thomas Jay Oord (PhD, Claremont Graduate University) is a theologian, philosopher, and scholar of multidisciplinary studies. He is an award-winning author or editor of more than twenty-five books, including *God Can't*, *The Uncontrolling Love of God*, and *Theologies of Creation*. He served for over a decade as professor at Northwest Nazarene University. Oord is known for his contributions to research on love, open and relational theology, issues in science and religion, and freedom for transformation.

John C. Peckham (PhD, Andrews University) is professor of Theology and Christian philosophy at Andrews University. Peckham has written a number of books, most recently *Canonical Theology: The Biblical Canon, Sola Scriptura, and Theological Method.* Previously, *The Love of God: A Canonical Model* won IVP's Readers' Choice Award and his dissertation, *The Concept of Divine Love in the Context of the God-World Relationship* won the outstanding dissertation award in 2012.

A. Chadwick Thornhill (PhD, Liberty Baptist Theological Seminary) is chair of biblical and theological studies and associate professor of apologetics and biblical studies for the Rawlings School of Divinity at Liberty University. He is the author of *The Chosen People* and *Greek for Everyone.*

General Index

affectivity, 9, 11, 14, 17, 19-20, 43-44, 54, 59-61, 64-66, 71, 81, 87-88, 91, 93-94, 98-102, 106, 108-11, 118-19, 130, 134, 138-39, 145 154, 156, 159, 162, 168
analogical language, 33-34, 44, 48-49, 54, 59, 82, 95-96, 98-99, 103, 106-9, 111, 113, 117-18, 120, 143, 153, 168-69
Anselm, 18-19, 134, 135, 139
anthropopathic language, 4, 34-36, 54, 59, 60-61, 94-98, 104, 108, 133, 148, 167
apophatic theology, 39, 71-72, 85-86, 105, 143, 148, 168
Aquinas, Thomas, 16, 21, 24-26, 30-32, 104, 134, 135, 140
Arianism, 10, 111
Arminius, James, 36
aseity, 18-23, 39, 44-45, 48, 51, 127, 167
Athanasius, 10
Athenagoras, 9
Augustine, 9-10, 137
Baines, Ronald S., 8, 14
Baloian, Bruce, 90
Barth, Karl, 20
Bauckham, Richard, 112, 132
Bavinck, Herman, 18, 33
Bonhoeffer, Dietrich, 55, 101, 135
Boyd, Gregory A., 135
Brueggemann, Walter, 61, 130
Calvin, John, 34, 95

Carson, D. A., 88-89
Charnock, Stephen, 27
Cobb Jr., John B., 135
Cone, James, 139
Crammer, Thomas, 13
creator-creature distinction, 20, 39, 48, 52, 66, 79, 81, 88, 95, 98-99, 102, 106, 113, 114-17, 120, 127, 156, 158, 168
Creel, Richard, 87
Culpepper, Gary, 88, 103
Cyril of Alexandria, 10, 68-69, 77, 80
Dawkins, Richard, 64
divine aseity, 17, 18-23, 24, 28, 35, 44-45, 48, 51, 127, 128, 147, 159, 160, 167
divine immutability, 35, 44-45, 47, 51, 57, 73, 79, 93, 104, 107, 137, 154, 162
divine relationality, 47, 48, 93, 124
divine simplicity, 15, 17, 18, 26-28, 39, 44-45, 48, 167
divine transcendence, 51, 66-68, 76-77, 79, 81, 99, 106, 143
Docetism, 10, 111
Dodds, Michael J., 30
Dombrowski, Daniel, 142
Dorner, Isaak August, 135
Duby, Steven, 23-24, 26
Dunning, H. Ray, 135
Emery, Gilles, 104
Feser, Edward, 50

Fiddes, Paul, 135
Fretheim, Terence, 97, 130, 136
Fritsch, Charles T., 61, 102
Gavrilyuk, Paul L., 6, 8, 10, 57-58, 71, 80-81, 102, 104-7, 111-12, 118, 126
Gill, John, 35
Goldingay, John, 90, 130
Gondreau, Paul, 36
Graetz, Naomi, 63
Griffin, David Ray, 142
Harnack, Adolf von, 6, 57
Hart, David Bentley, 14
Hartshorne, Charles, 137, 142
Hellenization, 6-11, 80, 81
Helm, Paul, 104
Henry, Carl F. H., 137
Henry, Matthew, 34-35
Heschel, Abraham, 129-30
Hillers, Delbert R., 64
Holloway, John Daniel, 130
Holy Spirit, 55, 67, 69-70, 72, 145
hypostatic union, 9-10
Ignatius of Antioch, 68
image of God, 65, 108, 133, 143, 156
incarnation, 4-5, 9-10, 35-36, 54-55, 67-69, 86-87, 99, 111-13
involuntary, 80, 85, 99, 102, 107
Irenaeus, 9
Islam, 129
Jensen, Robert, 107-8

John Cassian, 9
John of Damascus, 18, 27
Justin Martyr, 9
Kelle, Brad, 61
Keller, Catherine, 135
Kitamori, Kazoh, 135
Klubertanz, George, 16
Lee, Jung Young, 135
Lim, Bo H., 62, 64
Lister, Rob, 6-7, 19, 92-93,
    100, 104, 106
McCormack, Bruce, 135
McGuckin, John, 69
metaphysics, 14, 16, 18, 23, 24,
    26, 39-41, 42-44, 47, 49, 50,
    92, 104, 105, 121, 127-28, 141,
    155-57, 161
Miner, Robert, 16
Moberly, R. Walter L., 136
modalism, 10
Moltmann, Jürgen, 6, 19, 26,
    28-29, 45, 48, 55-58, 73, 81,
    100, 133, 135, 147, 168
Mullins, Ryan T., 44, 107, 113,
    137, 141
Nestorianism, 10, 68-69, 111
Nicholson, Ernest W., 61
Oswalt, John N., 91
panentheism, 146
paradox, 67-70, 72, 81, 84-86,
    111, 156, 168
Parunak, H. Van Dyke, 97
passivity, 14-17

Pinnock, Clark, 24, 57, 129,
    135
Placher, William, 132
Plantinga, Alvin, 100
pneumatology, 55, 67, 69-70,
    72, 145
Pomplun, Trent, 93
Pool, Jeff, 135
passion of Christ, 5, 6, 35-36,
    57, 69, 74, 76, 84, 92, 105,
    111-13, 133
prayer, 4-5, 21, 43, 55, 70, 89,
    108-10, 121, 131, 138, 158,
    168-69
pure actuality, 17-18, 22-26,
    39-40, 42, 44, 51, 167
Rocca, Gregory P., 34
Rutledge, Fleming, 112
Sanders, John, 104, 135
Sarot, Marcel, 133
Savoy Declaration, 13
Scrutton, Anastasia Phillipa,
    141
Second London Confession,
    13
Septuagint, 23, 60, 64, 102
Shah, Farhan A., 129
Silverman, Eric, 141
Sirvent, Roberto, 140
Smith, J. Warren, 69
Stott, John, 100
Studdert Kennedy, Geoffrey
    A., 58

Taliaferro, Charles, 107, 141
Tertullian, 9
theocosmocentrism, 145-49,
    157-58, 162-63
Thirty-Nine Article of
    Religion, 13
Thompson, John A., 91
Torrance, Alan, 132
Torrance, T. F., 135
Trinitarian implications, 10,
    67-70, 99, 120-21, 123-24,
    145-47, 158-62, 164
United Methodist Hymnal,
    13
Vanhoozer, Kevin, 95, 102,
    108, 147
Viney, Doland, 142
Ware, Bruce A., 93
Warfield, B. B., 104
Weigel, Peter, 26
Weinandy, Thomas, 13-14, 26,
    29, 38, 102-4
Wesley, John, 35, 47
Westminster Confession of
    Faith, 13
Whitehead, Alfred North,
    139, 142
Williams, Daniel Day, 135
Willis, John T., 96
Wippel, John, 24-25
Wolterstorff, Nicholas, 98, 135
Wuellner, Bernard, 15-16,

Scripture Index

Finding the Textbook You Need

The IVP Academic Textbook Selector
is an online tool for instantly finding the IVP books
suitable for over 250 courses across 24 disciplines.

ivpacademic.com